For You

Andreas Seidl

Handover of Power

Global Version

Volume 14: Education

Imprint

Bibliographic information of the German National Library:
The German National Library lists this publication in the
German National Bibliography; detailed bibliographic data
are available on the Internet at http://dnb.dnb.de.

© 2022 Dipl. Pol. Theodor Andreas Seidl

Cover: Christiane Ebrecht
Translation: DeepL, Cologne
Production and publishing: BoD – Books on Demand,
Norderstedt

ISBN: 978-3-7562-0138-9

Acknowledgements

My thanks go to my family and friends who have made me who I am today. Special thanks to all those who supported me in writing this book. I would like to thank all my classmates, teachers, fellow students, lecturers, demonstrators, activists, colleagues, companies and countries with whom I have had the privilege of sharing the experiences from which all the ideas in this book have emerged. I would like to thank the staff of Books on Demand for their kind helpfulness. I thank the citizens of Seligenstadt for the harmony and solidarity in which I was able to write.

Foreword

This policy concept contains a variety of proposals for possible political reforms. It can be peacefully and democratically adapted to any current political system of any state in the world, but also to political systems in families, clubs, associations or companies. Wherever humans make or submit to rules that manage living together, the following proposals can be helpful. Readers who find the proposals so helpful that they would like to implement them together with like-minded people can contact the author. The contact form on the last page can be used for this purpose.

Faults and defects
I ask for your understanding that this volume was not professionally proofread. I could only afford professional proofreading for the summary. Spelling errors and unfortunate phrasing may therefore occur. As soon as this volume has sold enough to pay for a professional proofreading, it will be done. After that, a new edition will be published.

English version
Please understand that this volume has been translated automatically. I could only afford a professional translation for the summary. Poor wording and spelling errors may therefore occur. In case of doubt, the German version shall prevail. As soon as this volume has sold enough to pay for a professional translation, it will be done. After that, a new edition will be

published. It was more important to me that no one in the world should have an information advantage than individual translation errors in the complete work.

References

If something has been quoted directly, it is set in italics. If the headings contain footnotes, the sources for direct and indirect quotations apply in the chapter for which the heading stands. Otherwise, quotations or source references are directly at the word or at the end of the sentence or paragraph. This book contains parts of text based on the Federal Constitution of the Swiss Confederation of 18 April 1999 (as of 12 February 2017), abbreviated to BV[1] and the Constitution of the Canton of Bern of 6 June 1993 (as of 11 March 2015), abbreviated to KV[2].

If the constitutional paragraph, or individual paragraphs thereof, are based in whole or in part on extracts from the BV or KV, this is indicated in a footnote. The references to the corresponding footnotes for constitutional paragraphs are usually found after the heading of the affected chapter and sometimes in the body of the text. Articles used in the Swiss constitutions are listed in the footnote with a number after the title of the constitutional paragraph. Example: §123 Sample title: BV Art.123, KV Art.123.

All internet sources are fully cited in the footnotes. They were last accessed on 30.09.2021. All literature sources are also listed in full in the footnotes.

All references to tasks undertaken by other ministries and described in more detail there are given in footnotes. Example: Model Ministry - 1.2.3 Model Chapter.

All footnotes are to be viewed in comparison to the respective source, so-called indirect quotations. Direct quotations are set in italics, but hardly ever occur. The source reference is intended to enable further investigation and to take copyright

---

1 This is not an official publication. Only the publication by the Swiss Federal Chancellery is authoritative. https://www.fedlex.admin.ch/eli/cc/1999/404/de On 14.12.2021

2 This is not an official publication. The Bernese Official Collection of Laws is authoritative. https://www.belex.sites.be.ch/frontend/versions/2420?locale=de#ART71 On 16.12.2021

into account.

Table of contents

1 Goals of the Ministry of Education

The ministry's goals are to shape education and research in such a way that learners and teachers are researchers at the same time and create knowledge together as colleagues.

Because every human learns differently and has different strengths and preferences, different types and methods of teaching are offered in which learners, teachers and researchers can democratically choose. Democratic and self-determined education is a goal of the Ministry of Education, which is achieved through the democratic management of educational institutions and the independent election of timetables and educational qualifications.

The Ministry of Education aims to ensure that as many humans in the country as possible are as highly educated as possible. On the one hand, this allows everyone the freedom of choice to take up any profession or follow any appeal. On the other hand, more educated humans are more likely to come up with innovative inventions because they know the state of the art and have enough knowledge in their specialist department to push the limits of today's science and technology. Most of the time, ideas emerge when different knowledge is combined. The Ministry of Education achieves this combination by allowing all members of all educational institutions to express their ideas and receive feedback on how the idea could be implemented. If the idea creators and their colleagues at the educational institution do not have sufficient knowledge, they can turn to their colleagues from any other educational institution. Last but not least, a population that is as educated as possible is essential so that the state and its organs can be effectively controlled and managed by the people. To this end, eligible voters must have sufficient knowledge to be able to understand policy deciders.

Another goal of the Ministry of Education is to create synergies between education and research. Educational institutions provide training for new researchers, jointly conduct research studies for each other and share their latest research findings with each other. In a research alliance, research projects of any size can be initiated as long as all those affected agree by a majority. Any individual educational institution that is professionally equipped to do so can participate in an alliance or open an alliance. The research tasks are carried out in a division of labour by all educational institutions capable of doing so. The research association acts true to the motto: One educational institution for all educational institutions and all for one.

2 Departments

The departments are divided into sub-departments and enumerations are usually considered as their individual units. Many tasks of some departments are completely taken over by other ministries as a service.

2.1 Central Department

Part of the Central Department is the Reception Office with the Courier and Mail Room, which directs all concerns, broadcasts and visitors to the appropriate place in the ministry.

2.1.1 Staff

The Human Resources Department is responsible for staff development and planning. For this purpose, it takes care of the recruitment of junior staff, intern and trainee programmes as well as the selection procedures for employees and special selection procedures for applicants with disabilities. For politicians and employees, the department prepares a job plan. In all its tasks, it works in voting with the personnel board.[1]

All other personnel matters are transferred to the respective ministries. The Ministry of Labour takes over the service law.[2] This includes the labour and collective bargaining law of the employees of the state service, remuneration, personnel administration of all careers and employees, flexitime, holiday and sickness file, working time with or without flexitime in part-time or full-time at the place of work or in home work. The Ministry of Infrastructure provides housing assistance for

1 Ministry of State Organisation - 2.1.1.1 Personnel board
2 Ministry of Labour - 4 State enterprises, 13 Labour Directory

all state employees.[3] The Ministry of Finance's Pay Office takes care of employees' salary, expenses, travel and relocation costs.[4] The Ministry of Health is responsible for the company medical service.[5] It provides occupational health management, deals with the treatment, education and prevention of occupational accidents, controls and provides occupational health and safety through the health auditors[6] of the Company Auditing Agency[7].

2.1.1.1 Education and training for the state service

The Ministry of Education maintains academies for state service in the colleges of all capital cities of the ministries. Depending on which ministry one wishes to work for, one attends the college in the respective capital city. Those who wish to work for several ministries consecutively or simultaneously must attend compulsory courses at the respective academy, if the job requires this.

Trainees new to the service or career changers can complete training courses for each type of service at the academies. Depending on the form of service, skills for behaviour, leadership, organisation, international diplomacy, personnel development and Information Technology are taught. Training courses for the specialist departments of the respective ministry can be attended by employees who wish to apply for another position in the state service. Whenever new technical devices are imported, affected staff receive the appropriate Information Technology training. All languages can be learned at the language learning centre. When foreign language skills are required for state service, the ministries send the affected staff to learn the foreign languages in the appropriate educational institutions.

---

3 Ministry of Infrastructure - 2.1.1.1 Housing assistance for state service employees
4 Ministry of Finance - 2.1.1.1 Staff remuneration
5 Ministry of Health - 2.1.1.1 Occupational Health Service
6 Ministry of Labour - 20.7.2 Health auditor
7 Ministry of Labor - 20 Company Auditing Agency

2.1.1.2 Childcare for state service employees

State employees can take their children to any nursery school of their election. They have a right to receive a place for their child from the Ministry of Education from the age of 2. If there are enough employees at the location who always have enough children to run a nursery school, it will be opened; otherwise, childcare places will be provided at the nearest state nursery schools. Sufficient free capacity is provided by the Ministry of Education.

2.1.2 Organisation

The ministries of media, security, justice, finance, labour, state organisation provide audit services for quality management in the ministry, evaluation of work performance, revenues and expenditures, as well as corruption prevention, sabotage protection and, if necessary, disciplinary matters.[8]

The Ministry of Labour regulates procurement law and ensures corruption-free state orders and procurement.[9] The Ministry of Finance organises the annual budget vote and ensures proper accounting in each ministry.[10] It regulates budget procedures, budget law, personnel budgets, departmental budgets, costs and cash management, and assists ministries in budget planning for the budget vote.

The Ministry of Digital Affairs supports the supply of Information Technology.[11] In voting with the Procurement Office of the Ministry of Labour, it takes care of the procurement, provision, maintenance and service of technical devices and software. Much of this is produced in-house to ensure data protection in information and communication technology. Information technology and digitalisation officers audit and advise the ministries. Digital appointment calendar

---

8 Ministries of Media, Security, Justice, Finance, State Organisation - 2.1.2.1 Audit services
9 Ministry of Labour - 6 Procurement Office
10 Ministry of Finance - 8 state revenues, 9 state expenditure
11 Ministry of Digital Affairs - 2.1.2.1.1 Supply of Information Technology

and documentation services are provided as well as a digital policy archive including a library.

2.1.3 Language Service

An interpretation service, general translation service and translation service for international law treaties ensure that state employees can communicate with affected persons in all necessary languages. All persons with a foreign language teaching assignment in the Ministry of Education are also called upon for translation work in the state service as part of their career. The Interpreting Service provides simultaneous translations and offers interpreters to accompany politicians or translation software that works through speech recognition and voice output through the People's Computer[12] . The general translation service first translates all necessary texts automatically and corrects the result afterwards. International law and international treaties are translated by specialists who also have knowledge of contractual clauses of the respective countries. For this purpose, the language service cooperates with the embassies of the affected countries.

2.2 Management Department

The Management Department is the minister's department. With his office team, he provides policy planning and analysis for his ministry and coordinates the relationship between the nation and the municipality through exchanges with his deputies in the municipalities. He initiates cooperation with other ministries or citizens in committees and is supported by the Ministry of State Organisation.
The Ministry of Media Affairs, through its media service, provides press and public relations for the ministry, moderates civil dialogue, trains or provides a spokesperson for the minister, writes speeches and texts on request, and ensures the implementation of conferences and events.[13]

---

12 Ministry of Digital Affairs - 13.6 People's Computers
13 Ministry of Media Affairs - 2.2.1.1 Media Service

The Ministry of Digital Affairs is responsible for digital management and thus provides departmental management. It automatically produces business statistics, staff surveys and the current state of research through statistics. It automatically forwards proposals to the affected or empowered state employees. In document management, it ensures digitalisation and that ministries share forms with each other.[14]

2.3 Education Department

The Education Department ensures the operation of the central education system, the guarantee of academic freedom and funding through revenues from the educational institutions and tax money. In cooperation with the educational institutions, it sets the learning objectives and coordinates the inner research cycle between the educational institutions. In cooperation with the educational institutions and the ministries of labour and innovation, it draws up the curriculum in a committee and invites suitable representatives from sectoral associations of all economic forms.

It supervises the Education Authority, Examinations Office and the Institute of Education and develops draft legislation on requirements and services for teachers. It cooperates with the Examinations Office, the Foreign Office[15] and the Employment Office[16] to recognise qualifications. It coordinates cooperation between educational institutions and companies and establishes contact with the ministries of economy. It coordinates the alliance between educational institutions for research and development and works together with the Ministry of Innovation for this purpose.

In cooperation with the Ministries of Security, Planned Economy[17], Social Market Economy[18], Family, Infrastructure and Health, it ensures the operation of the People's Service. In cooperation with the Ministries of Media and Digital Affairs,

---

14 Ministry of Digital Affairs - 2.1.2.1 Digital Service
15 Ministry of Foreign Affairs - 4.6 Foreign Office
16 Ministry of Labour - 12 Employment Office
17 Ministry of Planned Economy
18 Ministry of Social Market Economy

it operates the Knowledge Directory[19] and the opportunities for free education.

2.4 Department for Educational Institutions

The Department for Educational Institutions ensures harmonisation between educational institutions and the effective use of their differences. It formulates the draft laws for the Minister of Education on how minors, learners, teachers and researchers work together in educational institutions. With the Company Auditing Agency, it monitors their compliance. In cooperation with the Ministry of Justice, it ensures the admissibility of punitive measures and deciders by the education courts.

It operates the Education Directory in cooperation with the Ministry of Digital Affairs and ensures the integration of the necessary data from and into the Research, Ideas, Labour and Knowledge Directories.[20] It guarantees learners, teachers and researchers their rights and receives complaints directed against the Education Authority or the Examinations Office. It forwards motions addressed to the Minister of Education by learners, parents, teachers and researchers from their councils and committees.

It supervises special schools, nursery schools, primary schools, comprehensive schools and colleges. It provides conditions for easy entry and smooth transfer between educational institutions and their cooperation. In cooperation with the Ministry of Planned Economy, it ensures the operation of the special nursery school, special primary school and boarding school. With the Ministries of Innovation and Foreign Affairs, it ensures progressive and cross-border teaching, research and development through the colleges.

---

19 Ministry of Digital - 12 Directories
20 Ministry of Innovation - 5.3 Research Directory, 8 Ideas Directory, Ministry of Labour - 13 Labour Directory

3 Tasks of the Ministry of Education

The ministry's task, in the spirit of subsidiarity, is to grant the educational institutions as much autonomy as possible to carry out the tasks they can best do themselves. Tasks that can be done better centrally are taken over by the Ministry of Education. To this end, it maintains authorities such as the Education Authority, Examinations Office and the Institute of Education, through which it also provides services for teachers and learners.

The Ministry of Education is responsible for coordination with other ministries whenever cooperation is regular or requests come from educational institutions, ministries or companies. This includes, in particular, the preparation of curricula for all educational institutions.

The ministry's tasks also include providing free education wherever educational institutions reach their limits. The adult education centres and digital education with the help of the Knowledge Directory serve to offer and demand any knowledge at any time.

4 Education system[21]

The Ministry of Education guarantees all nationals a lifelong right to education and research. To this end, it coordinates all its educational institutions in order to always be able to offer sufficient capacities. The education system is designed to carry out the tasks of education and research simultaneously through the cooperation of both sectors. Learners are always researchers who repeat past experiments in order to arrive at the same research results. This has a special potential for basic research and the continuous improvement of teaching and research.

The education system consists of a central and a decentralised level. The central level is taken over by the Ministry of Education and decides everything there that is generally binding throughout the country. The decentralised level is taken over by the educational institutions, where they decide everything that is necessary to adapt the central requirements

---

21 §17,1 Right to education and research: BV Art.19

to the local needs of their learners, teachers and researchers. The responsibility lies with the management of the educational institutions in voting with the deputy minister of education in their municipality.

4.1 Scientific freedom[22]

It is crucial that all learners, teachers and researchers are so free that they can express all research ideas and suggestions for improvement, try them out and, if successful, share them with all those affected. State requirements for science, research and teaching are limited to setting priorities in order to promote certain research areas for urgent societal challenges. Under no circumstances may research results or test procedures be influenced in order to make the result turn out in a certain way. All interpretations of science are free to be marked as true or false only by verifiable methods. For all results that allow a deviation, the probability of the deviation must be mentioned. Interpretations that are not verifiable must be marked as such. Only through the freedom of scientific teaching and research can impartial training be guaranteed. In this respect, freedom of science applies as a duty of the teachers and a right of the learners, who can check this and report violations.

4.2 Central education system[23]

The Ministry of Education ensures that humans in the education system receive high quality training without harm. High quality is set through curricula that learners must prove in examinations and teachers must prove in examination marks and learner surveys. To ensure that the education space in the country remains permeable, this evidence and proof is provided in the same way throughout the country. What skills are needed across the country for survival at the current state of the art is decided by the Ministry of Education in voting with the Ministries of Labour and Innovation in a committee[24] .

22§18 Academic freedom: BV Art.20, KV Art.21
23§176,1,3 Education area: BV Art. 61a
24Ministry of State Organisation - 9.6 Committee

The central education system is organised like a democratic community of researchers discovering the world together. Schools and colleges work within the national network for teaching and research. The requirement is to meet the learning goals. They represent the qualifications needed to survive self-determinedly in today's society, which includes gainful employment, for which one must be qualified. For this, all the necessary qualifications are translated centrally in the Ministry of Education into a degree that fits the job role.

Curricula are democratically adopted by the research community by involving all participants in the development process. This includes learners, teachers, researchers and associations of companies and organisations where learners will work after graduation. The Ministry of Education facilitates the collaboration. Since curricula and learning goals are considered state requirements, the people always have a say here. Therefore, curricula can also be determined by a quorum through a People's Committee.

Grades in numbers are there to see how much you can still learn. They are available on request and in all central performance records. A minimum level determines how much you have to learn at least in order to be able to do something. If the minimum is not mastered, the performance record is considered failed and must be repeated.

4.3 Financing[25]

Education is entertainment for the curious human being and should be financed by its innovative power through taxes, not through contributions or fees. The financing of the education system is managed through taxes and profits. The profits come from the cooperation with companies or People's Innovation Company. They must not be used for specific purposes, but serve the entire education system. In particular, vocational training must not displace general education in order to collect more profits.

Educational institutions are Tax-funded for minors and nationals. The people determine the amount in the annual budget vote, but cannot dispose of the profits generated by

25 §178 Training contributions: BV Art.66

educational institutions.

Training contributions are only levied at state educational institutions for foreigners of age of majority and companies in the Free Market Economy[26] that require special training courses. The amount of the training contributions depends on the democratic decision of the respective educational institution. It must charge at least a cost-covering amount and pay it to the Ministry of Education. Should there be capacity bottlenecks, there may only be waiting lists for foreigners of age of majority and companies of the Free Market Economy.

4.4 Learning objectives of the education system

The educational system has educational institutions that are designed to enable humans to reach an ever higher level of knowledge when they attend them. In nursery schools, children learn to master their own bodies and how they create their rhythm of life with food, clothing, excretions, sleep and free play. Research is done on how humans develop, learn, play and whether regularities can be identified. In primary school, knowledge of the past is learned and research is done on how to survive in a civilisation without electricity. In comprehensive school, the knowledge of the present is learned and explored, how to survive in a civilisation with internet. In the colleges, the knowledge of the future is taught and how to create knowledge. Research is done on how human civilisation can survive even if one day the earth no longer exists.

4.4.1 Research circuit

The continuous improvement of research and teaching is determined by the inner and outer research cycles and finds its limits in the inviolability of human life and animal and plant ecosystems. The inner research cycle explores how which human can learn the fastest, forget the least, successfully apply what has been learned and invent the most successful ideas. All educational institutions are in this circuit.

The outer research circuit researches the environment and

26Ministry of Free Market Economy

its use by humans. All educational institutions, ministries, researching and training companies and the population are in this circuit. In order for all humans to be able to comprehend the findings, the methods that led to the knowledge and the findings must be published in a form that can be understood by all humans.

4.4.2 Curriculum development[27]

The ministries of education, labour and innovation draw up the curriculum together with representatives of the business community and the educational institutions.[28] The creation of the curriculum is like a direct or representative legislative process.[29] The committee follows the direct legislative process. The representative form is chosen by default, in which the Minister of Education convenes a council that prepares a proposal. This proposal is then given to all learners, teachers and researchers in the educational institutions for revision, to be subsequently accepted or rejected by the Minister of Education.

The council, which is convened by the Minister of Education and of which he is the leader, has the following members: Firstly, a representative is sent from all party wings of the education party, chosen by the respective party wing. They present all the proposals of their working groups.

Secondly, a leader is selected from all subject areas of the colleges that train teachers. The selection is made by the Minister of Education. They draw up learning objectives and deadlines within which the objectives should be achieved. The learning objectives are based on what basic knowledge is necessary to be able to understand all further contents of a subject.

Thirdly, all sectoral federations send their leaders. The prerequisite is that a leader has already worked in his or her sector and has not only been employed by the association. They

27 §177,2 School system, §181,3 Vocational training
28 Ministry of Labour - 11.2.1 Necessary educational content, Ministry of Innovation - 6 Innovation through education
29 Ministry of State Organisation - 9.10.11.3 Direct legislation, 9.10.11.9 Representative legislation

are to add learning objectives with necessary qualifications for their appeals.

Fourthly, the Ministry of Innovation sends staff from the Innovation Agency. The Minister of Innovation makes the selection. They assess which curricula are forward-looking and close to the state of the art.

Fifth, the Ministry of Labour sends responsible economic auditors from the Company Auditing Agency[30] . They assess what economic impact curricula might have.

The council jointly prepares a proposal. The Education Directory publishes the process and all meetings of the council can be viewed via livestream. This first proposal of the curriculum is sent to all educational institutions. The written document is also available for download as an editable file in the Education Directory.

Now the teachers, learners and researchers from all educational institutions have the chance to change the text, delete passages and add new ones. In a teacher's conference, the file or document is handed out and everyone is asked to read the general part about offers for appropriate work and social behaviour and the section for their subject. Primary school teachers pay attention to what learning will come after primary school. Comprehensive school teachers pay attention to what basic knowledge is already available and what knowledge is to be achieved at graduation. Lecturers at colleges pay attention to which qualifications for which appeals are in demand in the content of the final examinations. After the comments have been made, the education submitters send the file back to the Minister of Education. He can accept or reject this second proposal.

If it is rejected, the process can be repeated, but this time it starts with the educational institutions and ends with the council. If the Minister of Education rejects this curriculum again, it must be drawn up in a People's Committee and put into effect by a referendum. All council meetings must be published simultaneously on Government Television[31] . Once

---

30 Ministry of Labour - 20.7.3 Economic auditor
31 Ministry of Media - 7 Government Television

the veto quorum[32] for this policy process reaches 30%, the curriculum must be created in a committee. The curriculum remains current until the repeal quorum of 50% is reached or the Minister of Education seeks a revision.

In the same way, a new educational programme can be established or an old one abolished as soon as one of the participants involved in curriculum development takes the initiative. Educational programmes are all educational objectives in nursery schools, subjects in school and study programmes in college.

4.5 Education Authority[33]

The Education Authority is located in the capital city of the Ministry of Education and has a department for each type of educational institution. In the departments, the performance of teachers is reviewed and their career paths are voted on. Teachers have to change jobs several times during their careers, sometimes working in companies, sometimes doing research in institutes and sometimes working for the Ministry of Education in the capital city. The Education Authority supports teachers in these transitions.

Learners can contact the Education Authority if they have urgent problems with a teacher, lesson content or exam results. Any complaints must be investigated by the Education Authority. If they cannot be resolved conclusively, the case is referred to the Remit Courts for Education. The Education Authority maintains its own school psychologists who try to resolve psychological problems of learners caused by teachers, learning or examination stress.

4.6 Examinations Office[34]

The Examinations Office is located in the capital city of the Ministry of Education and has a separate department for each subject area. In the departmental divisions, examination papers

32 Ministry of State Organisation - 9.5.14 Veto quorum
33 §176.2 Education area: BV Art. 61a
34 §176.2 Education area: BV Art. 61a

for central performance records and final examinations are drafted and sent to the educational institutions shortly before the examinations begin. Teachers from all over the country work in the capital city for 12 months. The teachers create the central performance record and final examination papers from the performance specifications of the curriculum. Later, they correct some of these exams on a random or targeted basis in all subjects and learning years. Targeted corrections are made when a new teaching method is tested.

All teachers must send all their learners' ratings to the Examinations Office. From this, testimonials are produced at the end of each term and sent to the learners' People's Computers. For underage learners, parents also receive the testimonials on their People's Computers.

4.6.1 Central performance record

In all educational institutions, central performance records are conducted once a year in each subject. Central performance records are tests for learners and teachers alike. If learners perform very well on average, the teacher's performance is very good.

The Examinations Office determines the dates when central performance records are held in all subjects. The period for the project exam and the dates for the written and oral exams are announced at the beginning of a school year. There must be at least 5 months between the announcement of the dates and the examinations. The dates are the same throughout the country. Teachers may not take leave during this period.

The scope of the examination varies according to the educational institution and increases with the level of education. The rating and grading is the same for all examinees throughout the country. It is not based on any average.

In the nursery school, these are observation sheets and games with appropriate rules for each year group. From primary school onwards, there is a choice of three forms of examination, namely a written exam, an oral questionnaire or a set project. The oral and written performance records are given at the same time. The period for the project exam also ends on the same day.

4.6.1.1 Project exam

The Examinations Office develops tasks that must be completed within a specified time period. The examination papers include a case description that clearly identifies the topic, the tasks and the expected end result. Notes are given if procedural requirements are necessary. The instructions and requirements may be more or less specific, depending on the team's own performance to be developed and examined.

In developing the tasks, the Examinations Office ensures that project results are economically or scientifically useful and saleable. To this end, in cooperation with the Company Auditing Agency, negotiations are held with companies and institutes to determine whether and which results from project exams would subsequently find a buyer or purchaser. If no buyers are found, the services go to the Planned Enterprises, state enterprises or to the research and development work of the colleges. The examinees whose services are bought receive a profit share of 1%. The rest goes to the Ministry of Education. The projects are examined and graded by expert teachers from other educational institutions. There are partial grades for individual performances and group performances. The examinees must describe all individual and group performances in a project report with text, pictures or video.

4.6.1.2 Written exam

The Examinations Office develops the task sheets and sample solutions for the written central performance records. The tasks are only sent to the educational submissions via the intranet on the day of the examination. At the primary school, they are printed out, handed out to the examinees, filled in by them, collected by the teacher and sent to the Examinations Office in an envelope. At the comprehensive school, the tasks are loaded into a computer programme which the examinees complete in the classroom on their People's Computer. The computer programme cannot be closed during the examination period, all other applications are automatically aborted.

In the room, five ceiling cameras are set up in the corners and centre of the room while the exam is being written. They send a 360° image in real time to the Examinations Office. The camera does not have to move. The fisheye effect with a high resolution allows a section of the image to be digitally enlarged. The video material including sound is stored on the Examinations Office server and automatically analysed. Algorithms look for conspicuous features that suggest an attempt to cheat and alert the invigilator in the room. If cheating is detected, a grade of 6 is awarded.

As soon as the tasks have been completed or the time has expired, all completed tasks are saved and sent to the Examinations Office. The tasks are automatically corrected and saved in the examinee's profile in the Education Directory. The examinee checks the automatic corrections, marks incorrect corrections and can request a human correction by a teacher.

4.6.1.3 Oral exam

The Examinations Office creates the digital questionnaires including sample solutions for the oral central performance records. It develops a virtual examination situation with simulated avatars and examination locations in cooperation with the Institutes for Education and Evaluation and the Ministry of Digital Affairs.

Learners must record the oral examination alone at home using digital equipment. All oral examinees stay at home longer on the day of the exam and conduct the same exam there alone and at the same time. Only after the exam do they go to class. The equipment consists of a helmet with integrated soundproof headphones and opaque virtual reality glasses and the examinee's People's Computer. The helmet is lent out by the school. They report to their People's Computer and visit the Examinations Office site. There you are asked to activate the People's Computer camera. The camera is automatically set to wide-angle mode and captures all faces in the field of view. All other persons are asked to leave the room immediately. As soon as only the examinee's face is recognised, he or she must hold both ears in front of the camera. Hair must not cover the area of the ears. The headphones each have a camera on the inside, including a microphone and a light, which is switched on as soon as the headphones are switched on and placed on the head. This is to be able to detect whether earplugs with radio are being used as a deception attempt. The cameras in the headphones film the ear during the test. The microphones record what the ear hears. Glasses must be degraded, contact lenses too. Based on the values for visual acuity stored on the examinee's Health Card, the image in the Virtual Reality glasses[35] is adjusted. A camera on the inside of the glasses films the eyes so that you can see what the examinee sees. What the examinee says is picked up by a microphone in the glasses. The screen of the Virtual Reality glasses is managed by the Examinations Office, as are the speakers in the headphones and the data connection with the examinee's People's Computer.

The examinee is asked to put on the helmet, put the headphone cups tightly against the head and push the glasses up to the eyes until no more light shines on the eyes. As soon as the camera in the People's Computer detects the headphones and glasses on the examinee's head, a QR code is displayed on the People's Computer screen. The helmet has a 360° camera on top that recognises the QR code and scans the surroundings for persons or attempts at deception. Should the examinee move almost out of the field of view of the camera in the People's Computer, he is asked to return immediately or the examination is aborted. Whenever a deviation is automatically detected, a warning is sent to the teachers in the control room, who are shown all the images from all the cameras pointed at the examinee.

As soon as the glasses, headphones and People's Computer have successfully connected for all examinees, the examination can begin. Anyone who is still not ready after 5 minutes, removes the glasses, headphones or helmet, a person enters the room or any other attempt at deception is detected, must discontinue the examination and take part in the written re-examination. The questions are displayed to the examinee and also read

---

35 Ministry of Digital Affairs - 13.6.9.1 Virtual reality glasses

aloud if desired. He answers orally and everything he says is shown to him in writing on the screen. Only a certain time window is given for answering all the questions. Once all the questions have been answered, one can read through one's answers again and make improvements, if there is still enough time. Those who finish earlier are shown a film, but are not allowed to take off their helmet until the time for all examinees has expired. The exams are automatically corrected and displayed as a provisional result at the end after the time limit for the exam has expired. Anyone who suspects faults in the automatic correction can ask the Examinations Office to have the results checked by a human teacher.

4.6.2 Testimonial

At the end of each semester there is a testimonial for the learners, which is filed in their profile in the Education Directory. Teachers of each subject must enter all grades or ratings for learners in a table sorted by subject and learner name by a deadline set by the Examinations Office.

The responsible teachers, the Examination and Education Authority, the learners and, until they reach the age of majority, the legal guardians have the right to view the testimonial.

In the nursery school, the evaluations of the observation sheets are given a pass or fail rating for each developmental stage in each developmental area. From primary school onwards, grades are used to make the rating more accurate. The grades are designated as follows: 1 means "very good", 2 "good", 3 "satisfactory", 4 "sufficient", 5 "deficient" and 6 "insufficient". Head marks for work and social behaviour are awarded from 1 to 6. The grades of a subject are given at the end of the half-year from 0 to 6 with one decimal place. Grades for performance in subjects may only be awarded on the basis of the subject; a pedagogical influence may only play a role in the head marks. In general, a subject is considered failed if the grade is 4.1 or higher. The courses of the subject that have been completed poorly or insufficiently must be repeated, which means that learners are downgraded by half a learning year or a whole learning year in that subject. Demotions are not foreseen for work or social behaviour, but attendance at special school is.

4.7 Institute for Education[36]

Educational research is conducted at the Institute of Education. It investigates which educational institutions and degrees fit which companies and appeals, which teaching methods are suitable for which types of learners, how satisfied learners and researchers are, what the quality of the performance of teachers, learners and researchers is, how this quality can be improved and at what point it is necessary to adapt staff and infrastructure to increasing or decreasing numbers of visitors. To promote quality, the Institute accesses data collected by the Company Auditing Agency as part of the quality assurance audit and conducts its own surveys and research. It receives complaints if the democratic self-determination of teachers, learners and researchers has been violated or if educational institutions with the same disciplines are treated differently. The complaints are investigated and in the case of a proven violation, a report is sent to the ministers of education, innovation and labour.

In voting with the Institute for Evaluation, units of measurement and methods of measurement are defined that may be used in education and science.[37]

4.7.1 Matching educational institutions and companies

For the cooperation of the educational institutions with companies, the institute continuously researches which sectors and companies go together with which fields of study and which year groups are suitable for which cooperation. The Institute develops questions for this and the companies can develop questions for this, which are sent to the Institute for Evaluation and included in the Company Auditing Agency questionnaires.[38] The results are used to search for companies

---

36 §180,2 Schools and colleges: BV Art. 63a, §183,2 Research and innovation: BV Art. 64
37 §252 Metrology: BV Art. 125
38 Ministry of Labour - 20.10 Institute for Evaluation, 20.8.5

in the vicinity of the educational institutions. The aim is that all educational institutions receive a list of companies that need the knowledge from their fields. In turn, entrepreneurs receive a list of all the educational institutions that provide and test the knowledge that the companies needed. The legality auditors of the Company Auditing Agency also have access to the lists through their auditing programme and can check companies whether they cooperate with the educational institutions or not.

4.7.2 Matching degrees and appeals

The Institute of Education is responsible for researching what schooling, training, further education and training are necessary to be able to work in the respective appeal. The Institute uses this data to create the educational pathways in the Career Pathway Planner[39] . The data is collected by the innovation auditors of the Company Auditing Agency in the course of audits of companies and educational institutions. Entrepreneurs indicate which qualifications are currently necessary for jobs in their company and will be necessary in the future. Employees indicate which teaching content has helped them a lot, rarely, never or at least once in their previous professional work. Learners indicate preferences of teaching methods and subject areas in exams. Data from teachers are collected through their entries in the Education Directory. They consist of curricula used, learning methods and examination results. This data is linked to the data in the Labour Directory. This makes it visible which curricula for which degrees are frequently or rarely found in which appeals and which grades and methods are successful where, with whom, and how.

Subjects taught in educational institutions and qualifications in job advertisements should be linked as well as possible. If qualifications are in demand in many companies, the related subjects will be included in compulsory education. Curricula of qualifications that often lead to unemployment are revised.

Questionnaire
39 Ministry of Labour - 13.4.9 Career planner

The Institute of Education reports such incidents to the ministers of labour and education with a proposal to revise the curriculum.

4.7.3 Suitable teaching methods for learning types

Not every form of teaching is equally suitable for educating humans. In addition to personal inclination, which is difficult to categorise, it is also decisive which type of learner a person is most likely to be. The auditory type of learner is good at remembering things he has heard. Lectures are suitable here. The visual learning type is good at remembering things they have seen, for example in demonstrations. The haptic learning type is good at remembering things they have experienced, for example in experiments. Learners take a learning type test every year and the Institute for Evaluation analyses the data. For this research, the Institute uses active teachers who have already taught different learning types using appropriate methods. These teachers perform their service at the Institute for a maximum of 10 years and then continue their teaching activities again. Learning successes of different learning methods are researched through the random and targeted examination of central performance records. The Institute works with the departments of subject didactics to research which age groups and learning types learn best and in which way. In particular, what content should be taught in-service or at school and how both can be combined in a varied way. For this purpose, all necessary data from testimonials, surveys, Company Auditing Agency examinations, profiles in the Education Directory and Labour Directory are brought together. This shows which learning methods learners use to achieve the best results. How to teach the subjects is researched by the colleges in the departments of subject didactics and invented and communicated by teachers on the fly. Teachers notify the Institute of Education of a newly invented learning method as soon as possible.

The Institute evaluates all results and gives out the most successful learning methods sorted by learning type to the state educational institutions every year. All results of the

Institute of Education are published on its profile page in the Education Directory.

4.7.4 Survey among learners[40]

The Institute for Education prepares the questionnaires for learners in cooperation with the Institute for Evaluation and sends them to them personally. It uses this data for a bi-annual record of learner and teacher performance to supplement the central performance record and testimonials.

Learners fill in a questionnaire on their People's Computer at the end of a semester or at the end of a course for each subject. There they indicate how they experienced the lessons and rate their experiences. The ratings can be given as 1 for "very good" or "strongly agree" to 6 for "unsatisfactory" or "strongly disagree".

The general questions deal with satisfaction with the educational institution in general, the variety of the courses offered, a sensible coordination of content or time between the courses, the support offered for courses and settling in at the educational institution, too strong an orientation of teaching towards company interests and too little critical discussion, as well as the number of company contacts. In addition, the desire for more freedom of choice or more requirements in the courses and whether the learner is thinking about dropping out of the educational institution is asked.

The questions on the learning situation deal with difficulties with the performance requirements in the subject, the professional qualification of the teacher, the empathy of the teacher, the adaptation of the learning method to the type of learner, orientation in the choice of course, finding learning and working groups, competition between learners, contact with other learners, the handling of teachers, the number of learners supervised by a teacher in a course, and the structure and preparation of the courses.

The questions on learning history record which subject one

40§188.3 Statistics. Weichenrieder, Alfons J., Clair, Lucas T. 2010: Questionnaire on student satisfaction of B.Sc. Economics/Business Education WS 09/10, Goethe University Frankfurt a.M.

has attended, how long one has been attending it and whether one is ahead, behind or on schedule in the subject. If one is behind schedule, one should indicate whether and to what extent it is true that the subject matter is too much, that one has been abroad, has failed exams, has been ill, has had too little money, has done internships or worked part-time, is employed or that the family situation has required it.

In the questions about the person, age, gender, learning type and the grade in the subject of the previous year are recorded. Learners also give a self-assessment here if they were able to remember and apply a lot of the lesson content despite a poor grade.

The last questions are open questions about what you liked about the course, what you thought was bad and what you could do to improve it. There are three text fields to answer the questions in writing. It is possible to insert an audio file or a video for each text field. Learners have the right to make hidden recordings to document repeated bad or good examples of the teacher.

4.8 Recognition of degrees[41]

The Ministry of Education coordinates with the Ministries of Labour and Innovation on the common objectives for qualifications.[42] The aim of the basic qualification is to be able to do only unqualified occupations for which no higher qualification is required, but at most further training. The aim of the advanced qualification is to be able to do all craftspersons' trades and to be able to do a part-time degree in these trades at a college. The aim of the college entrance qualification is to be able to aspire to all appeals and to be able to complete all subjects at college. If the ministries do not agree, the national Ministry of Education is solely responsible for the recognition of educational institutions and degrees.

The Ministry of Education is responsible for ensuring that the

41 §176.3 Education space: BV Art. 61a, §180.3 Schools and colleges: BV Art. 63a

42 Ministry of Labour - 11.2.1 Necessary educational content, Ministry of Innovation - 6 Innovation through education

degrees of all nursery schools, primary schools comprehensive schools and colleges as well as private educational institutions and foreign degrees are recognised or not. It is in close contact with the Company Auditing Agency, which regularly audits educational institutions and companies. During the audits, the requirements for educational institutions and the qualifications of those in employment are checked. For example, physiotherapists are licensed as soon as their qualifications have been checked by the Company Auditing Agency. Teachers only get their licence if they are in continuous professional development. They must attend training courses that offer degrees recognised by the Ministry of Education and have the testimonials of the degrees verified at the next Company Auditing Agency examination. If training or CPD is found to be deficient, it must be repeated. Anyone who fails to complete in-service training more than 5 times will have their licence revoked and will be subject to an occupational ban. This occupational ban can also lead to the closure of a company if the teacher is running a private educational institution.

4.8.1 Domestic recognition[43]

The domestic degrees are recognised at all educational institutions and by suitable companies. Through the cooperation of educational institutions and business representatives in the preparation of the curriculum, the degrees are already adapted to their needs. For all domestic degrees at state educational institutions, the Examinations Office prepares the examination papers. All examinations must be feasible in written, oral or presentation form. The examinees choose the procedure. The national standard for final examinations provides for the same tasks for each subject in all educational institutions.

Non-state educational institutions must have their distinctive degrees verified by the Company Auditing Agency, the Institute of Education and the responsible Examinations Office. Distinctive degrees deviate from the curriculum. Only

43§176.4 Education Space, §177.4 School System

qualifications of equal or higher value, such as the comparable state qualification, are recognised. Educational institutions planning to import a new degree must obtain permission from the Institute of Education and have the degree examined by the Institute and the Company Auditing Agency. During the audit, the Company Auditing Agency identifies the needs of companies and research institutes.

4.8.2 Foreigner recognition

Foreigners' degrees are examined in cooperation with the Ministry of Foreign Affairs before they are recognised. If a foreigner wishes to have his or her degree recognised, he or she must submit a motions to the Institute of Education. The embassies obtain the curricula and degree assignments of the affected country and send them to the Institute of Education. The applicant sends his or her testimonials and final papers, including assignment of tasks, to the Institute. In some countries, the examinee does not receive his final papers and their assignment of tasks. In this country, the embassy there submits a motions to send these data directly to the Institute for Education. The Institute checks whether all subject areas of the foreign degree correspond to those of the domestic citizens. Missing subject areas must be completed at domestic educational institutions. At the end, a regular final examination is held. If all subject areas and their scope are the same, no new final examination has to be taken.

In the course of international cooperation, the Ministry of Education can coordinate the recognition of foreign professional qualifications with other countries on an intergovernmental basis and works together with the Ministry of Foreign Affairs for this purpose. General recognition is then granted for qualifications from the affected countries. In the case of continental cooperation, states that are in an international union[44] between the Ministries of Education must reach a vote on the recognition of their qualifications in order to be allowed to operate a common internal market for

44 Ministry of Foreign Affairs - 5.8 International Union

labour.[45]

4.8.3 Need for degrees

Learners should know which degrees are currently needed. To do this, the Institute for Education synchronises the data of all companies, state agencies, learners and graduates. With the help of an algorithm, learners can access these data sets and calculate for themselves how many graduates will graduate with them and how many jobs will become available at that time, whether because employees are retiring or new jobs are being created.

The auditors of the Company Auditing Agency for Business and Innovation determine on behalf of the Ministry of Education which degrees are required by the companies. On the one hand, this includes the content of school or university education that is needed to do a certain job. On the other hand, how many jobs will be needed in which sector in the future. Through the teachers, this information is passed on to the learners. As a steering mechanism for degrees that are in short supply, companies are allowed to pay out bonuses per semester to learners in the affected elective subjects, advanced courses or degree programmes.

4.9 Education through work[46]

By enabling learners to apply what they have learned directly to the work that suits them, the learning process is reinforced in a sustainable way and at the same time the education system is involved in creating value through productive human capital.

---

45 Ministry of Foreign Affairs - 4.7 Embassies, 6.4.3.3 Services, 6.4.12 Continental Union Education Policy, 6.4.12.2 Single Education Area, 7.3.8 International Education Policy, 7.3.12.2 International Cooperation in VET
46 §181.2 Vocational education and training: BV Art. 63

4.9.1 Cooperation between educational institutions

All educational institutions work together to make transitions as easy as possible for learners. Educational submissions undertake joint excursions, host joint events and run joint projects. Learners are involved in the planning and implementation. The management of the affected educational institutions only limits the budget or the safety concept. In addition to joint leisure activities, there is also cooperation in which older learners provide honourary services for younger learners, thus saving personnel costs in the education system. Regular visits are established for this cooperation.

4.9.1.1 Nursery school & primary school

When the pre-school children from the nursery school visit the primary school, they take part in lessons that they already understand without being able to read or do maths. At the end of a lesson morning, there is a joint offering in the afternoon, which the children vote on. These days can be repeated if the children vote for it, or extended over a week. The exchange does not take place at the same time with all children. The primary school children are in the nursery school for up to 7 days and lead a game or project themselves or play along. Gradually, about 10 children from the primary school and nursery school are exchanged every week throughout the year. Only children from the first to third class level and the pre-school children take part in the exchange. During the summer holidays, all preschoolers attend holiday care at the primary school together with the primary school children for at least one week.

4.9.1.2 Primary school & comprehensive school

Primary school pupils from the fourth grade visit the comprehensive school in groups of 10 persons one after the other for a fortnight and one day, but not consecutively. On the first day of the visit, each primary school pupil is assigned to a comprehensive school pupil from the ninth learning year and accompanies him/her for a day. The primary school pupil is shown around and shown the school. The routes are predetermined so that everyone sees everything.

In the first week, primary school pupils attend the fifth learning year for one week. They attend all different types of lessons in different subjects and can make this choice themselves. For example, in maths this would be project teaching, in history frontal teaching and in all other subjects free learning.

The second week the primary school pupils have to design their own timetable via the Education Directory. They may attend all courses from the fifth to the thirteenth learning year within this week.

If a primary school pupil has the election to attend more than one comprehensive school, a visit day is held at each of these comprehensive schools. The two weeks can be spent at up to two comprehensive schools, so that only one week is spent at each comprehensive school.

The comprehensive school students in the ninth learning year regularly visit the primary schools in the afternoon and take over homework supervision or lead afternoon care activities and projects. The number of hours per year for each comprehensive school student varies depending on how many primary school children there are in the area and how many comprehensive school students there are in the ninth learning year. A digital duty roster[47] , accessible through the Education Directory, helps comprehensive school pupils sign up for afternoon care duty rosters. If a position has already been filled, it is indicated when the position will become available again.

During the summer holidays, all primary school pupils in the fourth class level and comprehensive school pupils in the fifth learning year spend at least one week in holiday care at the local youth centre.

---

47 Ministry of Planned Economy - 7.6.1 Digital duty roster

4.9.1.3 Comprehensive school & college

The comprehensive school students in their final years have to visit a college for 2 weeks each in their last two summer holidays. For their first day, they are assigned a student to spend the day with who shows them around the college and how to make a timetable. After that, comprehensive school students can attend any course at the college for a week.

The college students give private tuition during their semester breaks for exam preparation for the final exams in the comprehensive schools. These exam preparations always take place during the semester break after the winter semester and during the school holidays after the winter break. The premises of the schools and colleges are open to pupils and students for exam preparation. In addition, college students can offer play, work and research communities in consultation with the comprehensive school management in the afternoons during school hours.

4.9.2 Cooperation between educational institutions and companies[48]

Companies from the Planned Economy and Social Market Economy can be obliged to cooperate with educational institutions. Barter Economy[49] and Free Market Economy companies can apply to the Ministry of Education. The education system thus creates an opportunity for the promotion of young talent by companies and their own revenues.

4.9.2.1 Nursery schools and companies

The nursery school has career days. On these days, a parent comes to the nursery school and tells what he or she does for a living. On another day, voluntary children from the nursery school then visit the company where the parent works. Career days must take place at least once a year.

---

48 §180,6,7 Schools and colleges: KV Art.44
49 Ministry of Barter Economy

4.9.2.2 Primary schools and companies

In the primary school, there are regular classroom visits by employees of the municipal enterprises and excursions to the town hall and to state enterprises. The aim is that every primary school child should have experienced all municipal state services. Content is already included in the curriculum so that content learned in class can be experienced in daily use. All ministries are obliged to cooperate.

4.9.2.3 Comprehensive schools and companies

In the comprehensive school, classroom visits by entrepreneurs or their employees are carried out in each subject, as well as partial or complete production of goods or services for these companies. The participants either arrange the contacts themselves or the Company Auditing Agency proposes several contact options, one of which must be selected.

The work orders of companies at comprehensive schools are already defined in the curriculum and sorted from which learning years of which subjects which order can be taken over and which teaching content learned is supplemented at the same time. State-owned companies can be obliged to have some or all of their production manufactured in educational institutions. Companies of the economic forms may do so voluntarily. The companies must not suffer any disadvantages as a result. Additional costs due to cooperation with educational submissions are calculated by the Company Auditing Agency's economic auditors and deducted from the learners' wages. Learners will be paid at least the Social Market Economy minimum wage.[50] 10% is also deducted from learners' wages as a profit share for the Ministry of Education. The weekly working hours of a comprehensive school learner may not exceed 10 hours per week.

At the beginning, employees of the company visit the classes and teach the comprehensive school pupils what they have to do in the production process. Depending on the possibility, the production of goods or services takes place on the premises

---

50 Ministry of Social Market Economy - 9.3.1 Minimum wage

of the school or the company. If it takes place at the company, the entrepreneur must provide transport to and from school. If the production takes place at the school, the company must provide for the supply of tools and materials as well as for the removal of goods, services and residual materials. By using several comprehensive schools in the vicinity, manufacturing chains can also be established.

During production, the performance must be tested by the company. Learners who prove to be particularly capable in this process can be offered a traineeship or a job.

4.9.2.4 Colleges and companies

Entrepreneurs and their employees give individual lectures and lead individual appointments of seminars at the colleges. There they can present their work or explain and instruct work assignments. At colleges, every course of study must also be part-time. Whether work is done during the entire period or only during the semester breaks is left up to the colleges. The colleges conclude cooperation agreements with surrounding companies in Planned Economy and Social Market Economy, especially with People's Innovation Company. Performance records and final theses can be orders placed with the college by companies for which students have reported voluntarily.

The weekly working hours of a student may not exceed 20 hours per week during the lecture period and 40 hours per week during the semester break. A student's wage may not be more than 10% below that of an otherwise normal employee. A 10% profit mark-up is only deducted from the student's salary if the student has obtained the job from the college.

Entrepreneurs have the option of either using the college's existing institution or having the students work at the company's location. If companies use the college permanently, they can also install their own devices there, but they assume the liability and costs for this. Entrepreneurs also provide the necessary logistics, just as companies do in comprehensive schools.

4.9.2.5 Production network

Several educational institutions and companies can join forces to form a nationwide production network to work together on a project until it is ready for the market or completed. Market-ready products are converted into an independent Social Market Economy company with its own production capacity as soon as profits are generated. 10% of profits are transferred to the Ministry of Education before tax deduction.

4.10 Education through research

The Ministry of Education is responsible for the use of educational institutions for research purposes during school hours. The Ministry of Innovation is responsible for the use of educational institutions for research purposes outside school hours.[51]

Learners should realise that all content in the curriculum has been researched at some point and that they experience these research results in a much shorter time. In order to be able to understand where knowledge comes from, active research is also carried out at as many educational institutions as possible and research results are shared with suitable other educational institutions in order to be able to use them or carry out further research with them.

This innovation support includes research projects originating from companies, ministries or even members of the educational institutions. Learners and teachers can develop their own ideas in small groups and drive their implementation. If the ideas are promising for society, they can be implemented through an alliance of educational institutions, companies and ministries in a division of labour and thus accelerated. In the sixth learning year, comprehensive school students have invention lessons and learn the path from the idea to the industrial property right to the product. All learners can also be inventors and develop research projects to advance their own inventions. In doing so, they receive expert advice from the teachers, because

---

51 Ministry of Innovation - 6.3 Promoting innovation at educational institutions

teachers are also scientists themselves. On the one hand, by continuing to research how to impart knowledge and also by returning to colleges themselves at stages of their careers to conduct research in their specialist department. Colleges, in turn, are in close contact with research institutes and researching companies. In this way, colleges become a hub for research, development and education and establish contact between educational institutions and innovative business enterprises.

4.10.1 Inventor advice

At all educational institutions there are forms for ideas on how something can be improved. All you have to do is put it into predefined categories, describe it and, if possible, take a picture of it. This form is then placed in a special box in the secretary's office and stamped daily. Teachers are required to empty this box weekly and make an appointment with the author(s). The form is identical to the entry form for an invention profile in the Ideas Directory. The completed Invention Profile can also be shared directly with the responsible teacher of a subject via their profile in the Education Directory to make an appointment.

In this appointment, it is discussed and explained whether research and development is still needed and how this could work for the submitted invention or innovation. This could be work processes or products. If necessary, the teacher will provide the learners with a space in the educational institution that they can use weekly for a limited period of time to develop the invention. If materials are needed, there is an order list that the Ministry of Innovation maintains together with the Ministry of Infrastructure. If certain materials or tools are not listed, they have to fill out a permit application, which the Innovation Agency audits and approves funds to purchase the necessary things on their own and send the receipt to the Innovation Agency. For other advice, they can contact the Innovation Office.[52]

---

52 Ministry of Innovation - 4.2.1 Innovation Office

4.10.2 Inventive activity[53]

As soon as a protectable idea is discussed in educational institutions, the interlocutors should film themselves with their People's Computers. As soon as it is to be talked about on a scheduled basis, a patent camera must be set up.[54] If the invention is further developed, the individual inventors and their share of the industrial property right can be examined by the innovation auditors.

When learners, teachers and researchers at educational institutions have an idea that could be eligible for protection, they create an invention profile in the Ideas Directory. Based on the information provided, the system automatically checks whether an industrial property right could be granted and, if so, which one. If an industrial property right could be granted, the invention profile is forwarded to the Innovation Agency. If the industrial property right is a patent, it is registered immediately, but no investigation or examination is carried out. If it is a promising patent, the Innovation Agency will take all steps to see if it could become a new People's Innovation Company.[55] For all other industrial property rights, the proposal is to file a fee-based application.

4.10.3 Innovative activity in the alliance[56]

The educational institutions can be used to research ideas until they become patentable inventions and to market these inventions or other innovative business ideas. The educational institutions decide whether to participate in the alliance by voting, which the Minister of Education can veto. Through the veto, he can oblige the educational institutions to participate or exclude them from doing so.

If a person in the education system has registered a business idea or an invention, all learners and teachers in the course or research group should first help to make the idea marketable.

---

53 §154.4 Tax reduction, §183.5 Research and innovation
54 Ministry of Innovation - 7.3.2 Patent camera
55 Ministry of Innovation - 4 Innovation Agency, 8.2 Invention Profile, 7.3.1 Promising Patents, 10 People's Innovation Company
56 §183,1,3,4 Research and innovation: BV Art. 64

In the case of promising patents, as many educational institutions as necessary from as many subject areas as possible help and form a research network.

Commercialisation can be done through licensing or production by educational institutions, companies or Innovation Communities[57] . Unless the Ministry of Innovation claims the prerogative to establish a People's Innovation Company, a company must be established in the Social Market Economy to take over the commercialisation as soon as the commercialisation is profitable. 10% of the profits of this company must be transferred to the Ministry of Education before tax deduction.

4.10.4 Research network

What is special about the central education system is that research projects can be carried out in a large alliance of educational institutions with suitable subject areas. The ministries of education, innovation and labour work together to implement research projects. The aim is to inform as many brains as possible about a research project, no matter how old they are. This should in no way create a compulsion. Only if someone happens to have the right idea, it must be discovered as immediately as possible.

4.10.4.1 Research project

At the beginning of the collaboration in the research network, a decision is made on a research project, which is selected from many proposals. All researchers may submit proposals, regardless of whether they are researchers at state or private colleges, institutes or companies. Via the challenge search engine[58] , all participants rate the projects on how much they would like to be involved in this research. The voting is not only about interest, but also about the material and personnel possibilities of being able to take on work steps in the project.

---

57 Ministry of Innovation - 9.10.1 Innovation Community (IC)
58 Ministry of Innovation - 8.4 Challenge Search Engine

An algorithm automatically calculates who can take over which work steps on the basis of data from directories and audits by the Company Auditing Agency and proposes it to those affected. Those who had selected several projects must now decide on one project. After this final voting, it is clear who will carry out which research project with whom and who will take over which work steps.

4.10.4.2 Division of labour

Each of the three ministries takes over one work step and provides the necessary personnel to carry out the work step.

The Ministry of Innovation provides part of the funding through the Innovation Fund and the Research Cost Fund.[59] The Innovation Agency ensures that the state of the art can be used and, if necessary, sends mobile Innovation Labs with the appropriate equipment. The Patent Office ensures that protectable research results are patented quickly and free of charge.

The Ministry of Labour is looking for companies that have their own research departments to place some of their personnel and materials at the service of the research network. Companies from the Planned Economy and Social Market Economy may be required to participate. The Ministry of Labour also manages auditors and advisors from the Company Auditing Agency to review materials, health and safety.[60]

The Ministry of Education, through its educational institutions, manages the laboratories and lab assistants. Whenever possible, learners work as lab assistants as early as possible. This is already possible from nursery school onwards, but can usually only be implemented from primary or comprehensive school onwards, because the necessary prior knowledge is only available there.

The Ministry of Education coordinates which subject areas of which educational institutions agree to participate in a research project that suits them. Participation is not compulsory and

---

59 Ministry of Innovation - 9.11.1.1 Innovation Fund, 5.3.1 Research Cost Fund
60 Ministry of Labour - 20.7.2 health auditor, 20.7.4 technical auditor

requires a majority of learners to decide in favour of a proposed research project.

4.10.4.3 Research in the classroom

No matter what the research project is, it can be assigned to any school subject or field of study. In this lesson, the research project is presented and a work step is carried out. This fulfils part of the curriculum. Teachers prepare the research steps so that the experiments are carried out in class or as an assessed performance record. Especially when accuracy and freedom from errors are important, research steps are taken as an assessed performance because they are then checked again by a teacher. In this way, the Ministry of Education provides the necessary data from experimental series and answers to the research questions.

If participants have an idea for improving the research process, contact is immediately made with the author of the research project. In this way, school children are already involved in actively creating knowledge, which makes the direct meaning of learning at school obvious, because all school knowledge was created at some point. All pupils and college students learning inland, as well as their teachers and lecturers, are then researchers at the same time.

The digitised libraries of all educational institutions, to which all learners, teachers and researchers have unrestricted access via their People's Computer, serve as the basis for academic work.

4.10.5 Prize competition

Since all learners can also be inventors, the local Innovation Agency does a prize competition every year for all educational submissions in their city hall district. All courses take part. The prizes are a course trip to a domestic theme park of their election for three days and two nights' accommodation.

4.11 Teachers

Teachers at state nursery schools, primary schools, comprehensive schools and colleges are multiprofessionally trained and educated. They take on different tasks at different stages of their professional career as a state teacher. They are employed in the educational institutions, Education Authority, Examinations Office, business and academia of their subject as well as in the appropriate professional department of the Company Auditing Agency.[61] This diversity ensures innovative, unbiased and experienced teachers of learners and researchers who can explain their subjects with many everyday examples. The training requirements and curricula are the same throughout the country. Teaching at several educational institutions at the same time is possible. Correction and rating of performance records are anonymous. Teachers are supported by the Ministry of Education in this and in the design of lessons.

4.11.1 Training for teachers

Teacher training is the same at colleges, so students can easily change colleges. The main subject consists of four compulsory subsidiary subjects, namely didactics, pedagogy, social psychology and anthropology. Prospective teachers at schools and colleges must study the appropriate minor for each subject they wish to teach later. For teachers who wish to work in nursery schools or in afternoon care at primary schools, the subsidiary subjects are not required.

The degree programme provides for 4 internships during the semester breaks, which must last a total of at least 6 months. They must have something to do with the subject the teacher wants to teach in the future. For example, a teacher of chemistry and language completes internships with a pharmaceutical manufacturer, in a plastics production, a library and marketing agency. Nursery teachers do placements in nursery schools, youth centres, children's homes[62] and leisure operators.

---

61 Ministry of Labor - 20 Company Auditing Agency
62 Ministry of Planned Economy - 18.1.7 Children's House

The study programme can also be done part-time, whereby students up to the end of the basic study programme are only employed as temporary staff. Career changers can do in-service training and get credit for suitable passed courses from their previous studies.

4.11.2 Hiring

The Ministry of Education advertises and trains staff as soon as the algorithm of birth rate, relocation rate, quota of foreigners and age of teachers indicates a need. In addition, teachers can indicate in their questionnaires that they need more staff. For example, if the birth rate increases, more staff will be trained and, if necessary, more buildings will be built. If staff are 5 years away from retirement, more staff will be trained.

The vacancies for teachers are published via the Ministry of Education's profile in the Labour Directory and linked to the profile page of the affected educational institution in the Education Directory. Applicants can send their application directly to the educational institution's profile. All applicants in whom an educational institution is interested are invited to an interview. This interview consists of a one-to-one interview with the management, an interview with the teaching staff and an interview with elected student representatives. The interviews are video recorded. The videos are available in the Education Directory to help members of the affected educational institution choose which applicant to vote for. Applicants who receive a majority vote are recruited.

4.11.3 Duration of employment

Teachers' employment contracts are open-ended. However, termination may occur not only after three warnings, but also in case of repeated poor voting or performance results. Teachers may be transferred to another educational institution up to 3 times at their own discretion.

The Examinations Office evaluates the teaching performance of the teachers via the annual central performance records in each subject. If there is an upward trend from an average of 3.0, the three-year observation phase begins. If the average does not change after three years to an average of 2.5 or less, which continues for at least two years, the teacher is dismissed.

4.11.4 Survey

Learners rate their teachers every six months in the Education Directory. The personal data is only used to confirm the voting right to rate this teacher and is not recorded on the questionnaire.

In nursery school and primary school, those entitled to vote on behalf of their children are still obliged to seek and take into account their child's opinion. From comprehensive school onwards, the voting right lies exclusively with the learners and no longer with the parents.

In the nursery school and primary school, parents have the option of having their children's teacher replaced by a 75% majority. As soon as this happens, the head of the facility must send a report to the Education Authority, which also includes a survey of the parents' representatives. The reports are reviewed by the Education Authority on a case-by-case basis and if there is a repeated violation, the teacher is dismissed.

In the comprehensive school and college, learners have the opportunity to rate their teachers every semester. In the survey, they can indicate whether this teacher should offer this course again in the next semester. If 75% vote against, the teacher is replaced. Once a teacher has had to be replaced 3 times in 2 different educational submissions, they are dismissed.

4.11.4.1 Questionnaires

The questionnaires for the learner surveys are designed and evaluated by the Institute for Evaluation. Learners can give ratings on a scale of 1 to 6 and express praise, criticism and suggestions for improvement in response fields.

The teachers to be rated must not be present during the survey and the filling-in process must not happen at school, but only in the intranet café[63] or at home on the People's Computer. The completed questionnaires are sent via the intranet directly to the Institute of Education, the Education Authority concerned and the head of the institution concerned.

Unpopular teachers can be transferred by the management to another course, grade or educational institution, or they can try to find swap partners among their colleagues via the Education Directory. Unpopular teachers should exchange with popular teachers what they do differently.

4.11.4.2 Recipes for success of popular teachers

Popular teachers share successful methods with the head of the educational institution. The head shares successful proposals in the network of institution heads. All teachers of all educational institutions have access to this network. Teachers share innovative teaching and learning methods through the Education Directory. Teachers at educational submissions work together with the departments for subject didactics at the colleges. Studies on successful methods are conducted on an ongoing basis. All grades and learning types of learners who have been taught using the method and how their performance develops over the course of their educational career are recorded. This gives the Ministry of Education an ongoing opportunity to see which methods have been successful with which learners. All social science data of affected persons can be collected from the directories of the intranet, anonymised and analysed. The results are published each year as a list of success stories in the Education Directory. The educational submissions can see there which methods were successful in which milieu, for certain personalities and learning types. In this way, every teacher can choose the appropriate method from a wide range of methods and try it out. All learners who use a method from the list of recipes for success automatically take part in the long-term study for this method. If they agree, career data will also be collected until they retire.

---

63 Ministry of Digital Affairs - 11.1 Intranet Café

4.11.5 Career path for teachers

Teachers spend their professional career mainly at one and the same educational institution, but must gain at least 10 years of professional experience in the fields of business, science and authorities and are released from their teaching duties for this purpose. In this way, teachers should always be up-to-date on the state of research and development and be able to find jobs for their graduates more easily.

This work experience is not acquired in one piece, but divided into 17500[64] hours and accounted for on an hourly account. The Ministry of Education decides how strictly the hourly account is handled. If there are staff shortages in state institutions such as institutes or the Company Auditing Agency, teachers have to go there first. A cap on the number of hours for each sub-sector is possible. If teachers perform poorly in one of the areas, they can avoid that area and work longer in other areas that suit them better. Teachers from nursery schools also work in primary schools and primary school teachers also work in nursery schools. This exchange can be credited to the hourly account at 25%.

The economic area is covered by class visits and internships. Class visits by persons from companies and scientific institutes that are suitable for the subject can be credited to the hourly account. Internships in professionally similar companies of the Barter Economy, Planned Economy, Social Market Economy and Free Market Economy must be completed for at least 2 weeks at a time. The internships must be completed in all four economic forms. How many hours per week are worked in which economic form is left up to the teacher.

The scientific area is covered by research experiments and scientific cooperation. Research experiments are commissioned work by scientists from state institutes and colleges that is done in class. They are usually studies on which learners and teachers are to test something. Research work in state institutes of higher education and ministries usually takes place at the college or in the laboratory of the student's own educational institution outside the classroom. Teachers can become

---

64 250 working days per year * 10 years * 8 working hours per day = 17 500 hours

doctorates or professors on a part-time basis after sufficient research work. This requires having worked continuously on research at one or more institutes of a state college.

The Education Authority, Examinations Office and auditor roles in Company Auditing Agency departments each last one year and are to be completed at a time. At the Company Auditing Agency, teachers can be economic auditors in an appropriate industry in their field, or technical auditors, health auditors and innovation auditors if they have the appropriate expertise.

4.11.6 Educational institution manager

The head of a nursery school, primary school, comprehensive school or college is directly elected by the learners and teachers from among the colleagues of the teachers of his or her educational institution. Any teacher may stand for election. In this election, parents are not entitled to vote, but their children are. The teaching load is reduced to 50% of the weekly hours and the salary increases by 20%. The deputy minister of education of the municipality in which the educational institution is located is above the educational institution managers.

The management is responsible, among other things, for the democratic governance of the institution and, in voting with the teaching staff, draws up a course catalogue for its educational institution so that learners can make their timetables.

4.11.7 Remuneration

Teachers are paid by the Ministry of Education for all working hours, even if they are in the business, academic or agency sectors. Outside remuneration is not permitted and is considered bribery.[65]

Teachers are paid a basic salary that can increase or decrease by up to 20%. The more good ratings a teacher has in the

---

65 Ministry of Justice - 8.14.3 Bribery of state employees

surveys and the lower the grade point average in the central performance records, the more the basic salary increases and vice versa. Facility managers get 20% more basic salary.

4.12 Ministry of Education services for teachers

The main service providers for teachers are the Education Authority and the Examinations Office in the capital city. These authorities each have a representative in the local office of the Ministry of Education in the town hall.

The Examinations Office produces one central performance record per learning year and subject as well as final papers. In order to be able to implement the curriculum, all necessary materials are ordered via the Procurement Office[66] in voting with the affected teachers. Materials specially created or compiled by the Examinations Office are proposals for oral and written exams or project exams, together with solutions, suggested grades, screen presentations, videos, anthologies of textbooks or specialist literature and press releases. Teachers can order these materials and use them in their lessons. A search team from the Examinations Office is constantly looking for new educational opportunities. It searches bookshops for promotional new publications. It contacts companies that want to send staff to educational submissions, allow company visits or collaborate in research or production with educational submissions. Screen presentations of new research from subject areas are created from information provided by institutes and colleges. Documentaries, feature films or shows that fit a particular subject are compiled as a video series. All information for which the right to copy lies with the state is also published in the Knowledge Directory in the appropriate subject area.

The Education Authority has its own substitute teachers who are deployed in educational institutions where there are currently absences. After 5 working days of sick leave, the substitute teacher holds the lessons. They are always on business trips and have a camper van as their official car. At the same time, they work as reporters for the Education Authority

66Ministry of Labour - 6 Procurement Office

to inform about innovative methods or untenable conditions.

4.12.1 Correction

Teachers are free to choose how they form their grades and which form of performance records they offer. However, there are clear requirements for the implementation and correction of the central performance record and final examinations in order to ensure comparability between all educational institutions. Examination papers come from the central Examinations Office in the capital city. They are carried out under video surveillance in order to be able to determine the individual performance without fraud.

4.12.1.1 Forms of examination

Central performance records and final examinations may be written, oral or a project. Written exams are written at the learner's educational institution and given to an other educational institution for correction. Oral exams are taken at an other educational institution in front of foreign teachers of the affected subject. Examinees visit the other educational institution for the period of the oral exam, the address of which is sent to them 7 days before the exam. As soon as the necessary programmes, People's Computers, helmets and Virtual Reality glasses are available, oral exams are taken digitally from home. Project exams are taken by teachers from another similar educational institution by visiting the examinees where the project is presented. All participating examinees must submit their individual performance on the project in writing to the third-party examining teachers. The more participants involved in the project, the more auditors there are.

4.12.1.2 Examiner

The examining or correcting teachers are chosen annually by the Education Authority by drawing lots. It is ensured that the teachers have the same qualifications and, if possible, teach the same year group in the same subject. In the case of written exams, only the secretary's office is informed of the address to which the papers are sent for correction. The names of the examinees are newly translated into numbers for each examination. Only the Examinations Office knows these numbers until they are returned. Then the list is sent to the teacher who is teaching, in order to assign the names to the numbers again and to return the corrected examinations.

4.12.1.3 Digital exams

Written exams or digital projects can be created on computers at the educational institution and sent via the intranet to the capital city to the Examinations Office for correction or examination. In file format, the computer at which the examinees work assigns an exam number that goes on each page. The teacher who teaches receives the list with numbers and corresponding names only after the correction. If the correction can be done automatically, there is no need for an external teacher. Automated corrections may only be made via the servers of the Examinations Office in the capital city. The programme for automated examinations is developed in the Examinations Office in cooperation with the Ministry of Digital Affairs.

4.12.1.4 Control

Teachers need to read through the written exams after correction to know what their learners have done wrong or right. For oral exams and project exams, they can watch the video. Collusion between the examiner or corrector and the teacher is prohibited. They will be punished with a warning. On a random basis, 0.2% of the total volume is corrected directly in the Examinations Office for each central performance record and final examination. How the educational institutions are selected, whether specifically or randomly, is left to the Examinations Office. After correction, the papers are returned and digitally archived in the educational institution at the end of each year. The Education Authority controls these archives for central performance records and final examinations on a random basis. If corrections have been made incorrectly, a warning is issued to the responsible teacher.

5 Educational institutions[67]

Educational institutions are in the service of the general public so that the people are sufficiently educated to be able to live peacefully with each other because they learn to understand each other. For direct democracy, basic education is essential so that government action can be understood and rewarded or punished accordingly. The Ministry of Education runs educational institutions that are managed by their managers, supported and controlled by the Examinations Office and the Education Authority. State educational institutions are free because they are funded through taxes. Education must not be religious or influenced by a politician. The Education Authority and the Company Auditing Agency check whether these principles also apply in private educational institutions.

5.1 Differences between educational institutions

Educational institutions differ first and foremost in the level of knowledge one must have in order to attend them. Only secondarily does the age play a role, from which the physical and mental abilities are sufficiently developed to be able to fulfil the requirements. In nursery schools, learners are taught how to develop their physical, mental, creative, innovative, emotional and social skills in harmonious cooperation. These skills form the basis for further successful learning in subsequent educational institutions and for building a sense of responsibility towards other learners, teachers, fellow

[67] §177,1,3,5 School system: BV Art. 62, KV Art.43, §176,2,5 Education area: BV Art. 61a, KV Art.42, §180,5 Schools and colleges: KV Art.44

human beings, animals, plants and the earth. From primary school onwards, rules of conduct apply to ensure harmonious learning, and violations are punished with non-violent sentences. Primary schools enable the learning of the national language, both written and spoken, simple calculations, household chores and local current and historical facts. The comprehensive schools form the universal knowledge of the realities of the country and the world. In the colleges, this universal knowledge is specialised in one or more directions. All citizens who have knowledge gaps in one of the areas can attend the educational institutions to fill these knowledge gaps. Children are required to attend primary school from the age of six and must attend comprehensive school until the age of eighteen.

The times of the holidays can be decided democratically by each educational institution itself, but the total number of holiday days is the same throughout the country.

5.2 Harmonisation[68]

Usually the Ministry of Education, in voting with the educational institutions, coordinates harmonisation between the educational institutions. In order to make it possible for learners to move while attending an educational programme and continue at another educational institution, the following agreements are indispensable. If the educational institutions cannot agree everywhere, the Minister of Education determines the requirements on his own. The age of school entry is six years everywhere. Compulsory schooling applies from the age of 6 to the age of 18. All educational units may last a maximum of 6 months. The same content should be taught in all learning years in all educational institutions. However, when learners attend which learning year and how long they stay there is up to them. Transitions of learners between educational institutions must be accompanied in order to ensure that they settle in as quickly as possible, otherwise harmonious learning is not possible. Harmonious learning without fear, shame and

68§177,7 School system: BV Art. 62, §176,2,5 Education area: BV Art. 61a, KV Art.42

misgivings is the ultimate goal for all participants involved, because otherwise the bad memories will be recalled in the brain together with the knowledge learned at the time. The result would be that one behaves worse in an activity than one actually wants to.

5.3 School law[69]

Every citizen may use his or her identity card to ask any state educational institution whether he or she may attend classes or take final examinations. The request may only be refused if it results in the maximum number of learners in a course being reached. Teachers determine this number before the course begins. Learners rate after the course whether the number could have been higher or lower. Citizens who receive a refusal must be told of another educational institution where a free place can be found and, if necessary, be put on a waiting list. Waiting lists automatically result in more rooms, material and teachers being made available. Waiting lists should not exist in specialist departments where there are labour shortages or where such shortages are foreseeable in the future based on demographic data. The future is limited to the average duration of the educational programme until graduation. The Ministry of Education receives demographic data from companies on when employees retire every six months from the Ministry of Labour. The Ministry of Family Affairs provides the data on births.

If all teaching has been digitised in the Knowledge Directory, the right to personal tuition no longer applies. On the other hand, participation in final examinations may no longer be refused and a longer correction period must be accepted. If the correction period exceeds 2 months, more teachers must be involved or employed in the correction.

The primary school leaving certificate may be repeated as often as desired. The three comprehensive school degrees may be failed any number of times, but only 2 times per year. All university degrees may be failed a maximum of 3 times.

69 §45,1f Welfare state: BV Art.41, §177,1 Education: BV Art. 62, §233,2b Unemployment services

After that, the course of study may no longer be taken at any domestic college.

5.4 Compulsory education[70]

Compulsory education applies to all minors between the ages of 6 and 18. During this time, they must attend classes. Classes can be held in state or private educational institutions. Public schools and parents who wish to teach their children themselves are audited by the Education Authority. All benefits that minors receive as part of their compulsory education are covered by child benefits.[71] If children decide they do not want to live with their parents, they can go to boarding school in the Social Village. This maximum external care does not incur any further costs either. The shorter the children are in an educational institution, the lower the care fees. To record childcare hours, children use their child ID card, which is also their People's Bank[72] card with child benefits and their student ID card. Attendance times are recorded on digital time clocks in the educational institution at the entrances and exits of the building. For example, children who live in the Barter Economy and are allowed to be taught by their parents do not use any child benefit at all during this time, but they do for the central performance records.[73]

5.5 Children and youths[74]

All private and state educational institutions for the care and education of minors must comply with the laws on the best interests of the child[75] . Teachers have a duty to support and protect minors. The support mandate means always taking enough time to explain things to a child in a comprehensible

70§177.8 School system
71Ministry of Family Affairs - 8.4 Child benefit
72Ministry of Finance - 11 People's Bank
73Ministry of Barter Economy - 16.4.3 Home-schooling
74§45,1c,1g Welfare state: BV Art.41, §179,1,4 Promotion of children and youths: BV Art.67
75Ministry of Family Affairs - 8.1 Children's Rights, Ministry of Justice - 8.4.4 Child Welfare Endangerment

way until he or she has understood them. The protection mandate means to warn children of dangers and to reduce scientifically proven modern dangers. For example, looking at a small screen for long periods of time creates myopia, so the use of mobile phones at educational institutions is only allowed in necessary situations that serve education. Climbing trees is dangerous but does not necessarily cause damage. The mandate to protect derives from the duty of supervision that parents lend out to teachers of minors.

In case of a possible risk to the child's well-being, teachers cooperate with the Youth Welfare Office and the Ministry of Education provides all necessary data to the Ministry of Family Affairs. Data that teachers enter about children in their profile in the Education Directory can also be accessed via parents' People's Computers.

To give families the election of how much they want to live with their children, afternoon care services are exempt from compulsory schooling, as opposed to afternoon classes. However, working parents can also place their children in all-day care provided by educational institutions from the age of 2, which is guaranteed on weekdays until the age of 18.

All processes in educational institutions must be democratic, so that children have a say in how they spend their time. Children should get used to democratic participation from the very beginning of their lives. In particular, this should promote the independence and social responsibility of the adolescents. Social, cultural and political integration is supported for the whole group, which democratically determines how they work together.

5.5.1 Parenting

At parents' evenings, teachers inform the parents of the minors they teach about the learning status, strengths, weaknesses and how parents could help. If group-dynamic disputes arise in a course, there is a group discussion with all participants, their parents and the teacher. If this does not help, punitive measures follow. If parents refuse to cooperate and thus endanger the child's well-being, fines or imprisonment can be ordered by the courts, or the children can be taken into state custody.

5.6 Integration

Integration through education happens when foreigners repeat their degrees in educational institutions, attend civil defence classes or study for the immigration test. There are domestic people at the educational institutions who are to be got to know each other during breaks and joint events.

Foreigners who cannot speak, read or write the domestic language or can do so only poorly are allowed to attend appropriate classes at the local primary school. They co-write performance records and can thus obtain certificates to submit to the employer or as an extension for the residence permit.[76]

5.7 Building

The buildings of the educational institutions are built and maintained by the Ministry of Infrastructure. New construction or deconstruction is based on the birth rate, which provides at least two years until the child is allowed in the nursery school or has to go to school at the age of six. For any new building, the teachers who will be working there in the future must be asked how the architecture should be designed inside and out. If a conversion, extension or renovation is planned, the learners must also be involved in the architecture and furnishings with equal voting rights. The building includes a playground with seating and opportunities to play and move around, such as climbing frames, storage areas to lend out toys or playgrounds painted on the floor for people to play on.

---

76 Ministry of Integration - 4.2.3.1 Naturalisation Test, 7.7.6 Civil Defence Education

5.8 Files

All data collected in educational institutions must be entered in the learner's profile in the Education Directory. On the one hand, humans, as owners of their data, should have all records about them in their profile and, on the other hand, the data can be scientifically evaluated anonymously by the Institute for Evaluation in Education. The aim here is to enable research into personalities and temperaments and developments. For example, a statistical evaluation can scientifically fathom the theories of anthroposophy.

5.9 Education Directory[77]

The Education Directory is created by the Inranet Ministry and administered by the Ministry of Education. It consists of profiles for all persons involved in the educational system and groups for all educational institutions and unifications active in the educational system.

5.9.1 Profiles

Every learner, teacher, researcher and other employee of the Ministry of Education is given a profile in the Education Directory. The profile is created by each person at the beginning of his or her career in the Ministry of Education.
As soon as children enter the nursery school, their parents have to create a profile. From the age of ten, parents no longer have access rights to their child's profile. Teachers and researchers must transfer the data from their profile in the Labour Directory to the Education Directory. The information provided in the profile corresponds to the information that is asked again during the admission interview with the head and is thus confirmed. The personal data is automatically transferred from the profile in the Persons Directory.
The learner profile also serves as a file in which teachers must make all entries. Teachers enter absences, grades, misdeeds and commendable incidents here. Leaders enter school changes,

---

77§188,3,9 Statistics

positions such as class or course spokesperson or head boy, and merits such as honourary service. As in the rest of the state system, the data collected about a person always belongs to that person. Deletion is prohibited, but any part of the data may be hidden from public view by the owner. As soon as state agencies access this data, the access with time, date, scope of the query, ministry and agency is stored in the person's Access Directory, viewable and, if necessary, contestable in court.[78]

5.9.1.1 Educational programme

Each profile lists which educational programme is attended by a learner, taught by a teacher, researched by a researcher or supervised by a Ministry of Education staff member. The educational programmes are labelled with keywords indicating what is taught there and in which sectors the knowledge is useful. This data is linked to the Labour Directory[79] and the Ideas Directory[80] . In the Labour Directory, this makes it easier for companies to invite suitable graduates and for learners to find suitable jobs. In the Ideas Directory, inventors can more easily find subject areas where they can learn the necessary knowledge or which could support them in necessary research projects.

5.9.1.2 Timetable

How a learner organises his/her educational programme is determined by him/herself through his/her timetable. Teachers determine in their duty roster, in voting with their colleagues and the management, when they offer which course. Learners can register for them through their timetable. Duty rosters and timetables are the same every week for a semester. Exceptions are excursions, holidays or public holidays.
Teachers specify in their courses what prior knowledge is required and whether a maximum number of learners is specified. Learners unlock more courses to add to their

78 Ministry of Digital Affairs - 7.5 Access Directory
79 Ministry of Labour - 13 Labour Directory
80 Ministry of Innovation - 8 Ideas Directory

timetable as their level increases. For learners who are unsure, there is a timetable for each semester that is automatically proposed to them. The Education Directory algorithm takes into account the learner's interests and previous knowledge as well as the workload of the respective courses.

Teachers must enter their duty rosters 2 weeks before the start of a new semester. Learners must enter their first draft of the timetable at the beginning of the new semester. During the first week, all events are attended where teachers present their educational content and learners can ask questions. By Friday evening at midnight, all learners must have revised their timetable. Then the algorithm calculates which room size is sufficient for which number of participants. If events are too full even for the largest room, all affected learners will be notified on Saturday and must revise their timetable. The revision uses a request and bonus system that comes from the ministry's digital duty roster for Planned Economy.[81] Basic supply services correspond to courses and Social Villagers correspond to learners. This is to avoid learners being unable to attend desired courses frequently or several times in a row. If the problem of such a shortage of desired courses occurs more frequently, a correspondingly large number of premises must be enlarged structurally or more teachers must be recruited who can offer the desired course.

5.9.2 Groups

The structure within educational institutions is organised in groups. Each educational institution is a group to which all profiles of learners, teachers and researchers working there belong. Among them, there are subgroups for courses, subject areas, year groups, student councils and education councils. The groups of which a profile is a member are shown on its profile page.

A participant in a course is anyone who has registered for it in his/her duty roster or timetable. Participant of a subject is anyone who teaches or learns it. Year groups are all learners

81 Ministry of Planned Economy - 7.6.4 Labour Choice / Labour Demand

who started an educational programme in the same year. Student councils consist of all elected representations for learners and teachers. Group members of educational councils are all teachers, learners and researchers who participate in the democratic management of an educational institution. Steering group participants are all managers of all educational institutions. The steering group is a group on the profile of the Ministry of Education, where the groups for the Education Authority and the Examinations Office can also be found.

The groups are used for sharing information, voting, rating and commenting. The groups serve to enable democratic leadership in educational institutions by allowing learners and teachers to rate each other and their joint educational projects. The aim of ratings and comments is to ensure that cooperation is mutually agreeable or improved. Each profile of a group has the possibility to rate other profiles from the same group and to comment on ratings. Each group member can create a post on the group page or open a voting in a group.

Each group can set up projects in which all or some group members can participate. The project groups are run as subgroups. Volunteers can form study groups to prepare for exams together. The study groups are also managed as subgroups.

5.9.2.1 Suggestions for improvement

All contributions and comments can be marked as suggestions for improvement. These contributions and comments, together with associated posts or profiles, are communicated to the affected management and the Education Authority. Suggestions for improvement that are not only discussed but also implemented are rated during and after implementation. If the rating is good, the suggestions for improvement, including the affected contributions, profiles and comments, are sent to the steering group and the Education Authority. A list of improvements is kept in the steering group. All educational institutions are free to try out the suggestions for improvement. As soon as the proposal is used elsewhere, it must be rated, just as products are currently rated in internet mail order. However, here the time span is longer and ratings are to be given every 6 months for a maximum of 10 years. One can give up to 5 stars and write a comment. In this way, a list of successful proposals is created over time, which, with a majority of those entitled to vote, also find their way into the curriculum.

5.9.2.2 Teaching videos

Learners, teachers or researchers can create teaching videos and upload them to a group. There, the teaching videos are reviewed by qualified teachers and rated and commented on by all group members. Teaching videos that have been rated well and do not contain any technical faults can be published in the Knowledge Directory if the creator(s) give permission.

5.9.2.3 Research projects

On the educational institution group page, all ongoing research projects are listed as a subgroup. New research projects can be created by group members as a new post, which is marked accordingly. All other group members can rate and comment on the new project. If enough volunteers are found, the research project can start and a new research group is opened, which can also be active at several educational institutions. If research projects are carried out nationwide, the number of those entitled to vote increases. Members of the affected educational institution have three votes, learners of that discipline have two votes, companies and nationals have one vote each. The research project must be assigned to categories and keywords. If none of the indicated words apply, a new word can be inserted, but this must first be confirmed by the staff of the responsible subject area. The costs for the research projects with the most votes are calculated and listed in the Ministry of Education's financial plan for the annual budget vote[82] . Alternatively, the amount of money can also be generated via the crowdfunding platform in the Ideas

---

82 Ministry of Finance - 9.5 Budget vote

Directory.[83]

5.9.2.4 Elections of persons

Heads, teachers and representatives of a year group, a subject area or an educational institution can submit their candidature via the Education Directory. To do so, they create a post in the affected group, which they mark accordingly. The contribution must contain an election programme in which the candidates connect their intentions with the office. The programme can be uploaded as text, picture, sound or video via the People's Computer in the group. Candidates compete in the election campaign, create contributions and comments, are rated and commented on. After the election campaign, a voting is created in the group and votes are cast within 7 days. Whoever receives the most votes is considered elected. After that, voting for the deselection quorum is possible via the profile of the elected person. As soon as 60% of those entitled to vote have cast their vote for the deselection quorum, a new election takes place.

5.10 Rights for learners[84]

Learners have the right to be self-directed learners. Only they have the knowledge of how they learn best. Likewise, they have the duty to communicate how they learn best. To communicate effectively, learners can participate democratically in the decisions that affect them. Educational institutions must therefore be structured democratically. This also makes pedagogical sense because it promotes democracy building. Learners decide how they can best learn alone or in groups. To this end, political structures and processes are created that correspond to those of the state.[85] The Youth Welfare Office, Education Authority and Examinations Office are supervisory bodies that monitor democratic procedures

83 Ministry of Innovation - 8.3 Crowdfunding Platform
84 §177.2 School system, §180.1 Schools and colleges: BV Art. 63a
85 Ministry of State Organisation - 8 Political structure, 9 Political processes

and intervene in the event of complaints or deficiencies.

5.10.1 Management

The leadership of an educational institution is assumed by the head, who is directly elected by all learners and teachers of an educational institution. Teachers or researchers can stand for election. The process of this election is similar to the election of persons, whereby the election programmes are drawn up by the candidates and the government programme is replaced by the conception of the educational institution.

5.10.1.1 Council of managers

The council of managers consists of the heads of all educational institutions, including private educational institutions, who, however, do not have voting rights for votes that do not concern them. The council of managers can initiate and promote joint projects between several educational institutions. It cannot impose requirements on individual educational institutions with which they do not agree. The council of managers meets once a year in the capital city to discuss education policy with representatives of the Examinations Office and the Minister of Education.

5.10.2 Teachers

The executive tasks in the courses are carried out by the teachers. Elections of persons for teachers take place at the change of semester and when new teachers wish to join the educational institution. All applicants are the candidates who develop their own election programme, which consists of, among other things, their preferred teaching methods. During employment at an educational institution, elections of persons take place at the beginning of each semester. The process of election of persons corresponds to the compilation of the learners' timetable. They vote themselves into the courses and thus choose the content of the course and the teacher. The duty roster is similar to the election programmes, where each teacher indicates when and how they would like to present which learning content. The pre-election corresponds to the first draft of the timetable. The phase between pre-election and run-off election takes place in the first week of a semester, where all teachers present themselves and their programme in person. The run-off election corresponds to the revised timetable that applies to the learner in the coming semester.

5.10.2.1 Teachers' council

All teachers of an educational institution are members of the teachers' council together with the management. It can decide on joint projects, but cannot impose any requirements on individual teachers as to how they should teach. Particularly in the case of pedagogical problems, the teachers' council can conduct a collegial case consultation for affected teachers. There is an exchange about successful teaching methods and new research findings in the individual specialist departments. The teachers' council meets once a week.

5.10.3 Student council

The student council represents the opinions of the learners and can therefore form different wings. All participants in a course can lend out their voting rights to voluntary participants. For this purpose, an election takes place once per semester during the second week of class, where the teacher has to wait outside the door within shouting distance. During this time, all volunteers who are willing to lend a vote go to the front of the class in front of the other students. Each of these candidates gives a short speech about what is important to them in the subject and what their plans are. Then all the candidates spread out in the room and the other students stand for the candidate of their choice. Every candidate who has at least one other student standing becomes a delegate and a member of the student council. As soon as a student wishes to have a secret election, everyone must write the names on slips of paper, fold them and throw them into a ballot box. The ballot papers are immediately counted by the candidates in the presence of all course participants. Everyone who receives at least one vote belongs to the student council. These elections can also be held via the Education Directory if the student council so decides. Only if the elections are held on the intranet can students lend out their borrowed votes to someone else at any time. Student council members who no longer represent votes will leave the student council. These elections take place for all subjects individually, so that there is a student council for each subject. All members of a student council elect a leader who is equivalent to the party wing leaders. Course participants can also lend out their vote to him. Every leader of a student council automatically becomes a member of the Education Party and can join a wing. The leaders of the student councils must be involved in all teachers' councils, but they only have speaking rights and no voting rights. If a decision is made against their will, they can seek a quorum among the learners and have the decision voted on in an appropriate committee.

5.10.4 Quorums

Each learner can cast his/her vote for a veto quorum once for each decision of a teacher or the management that he/she disputes. 30% triggers an agenda item in the teachers' council and student council. 50% triggers a committee.
You do not necessarily have to cast your vote for the deselection quorum. You can also simply change the course if you do not like the teacher. However, if you do not want the teacher to work at the educational institution any more, you can cast your vote and change the course or stay in the course. Voting is anonymous, suggestions for improvement and criticism can be voiced anonymously. If 30% of the course participants vote for the deselection quorum, they trigger a course committee, 75% lead to a change of teacher. The management must provide the affected course with at least 2 teachers for election within 2 weeks. If this is not possible, the Education Authority must provide at least 2 teachers for election within 4 weeks.

5.10.5 Committee

The committee is also used in educational institutions to make decisions together or to establish rules. It takes place as a course committee when all participants of a course, including its teacher, meet with equal voting rights at least once a month. The year group committee, which includes all learners who have joined the educational institution in the same year, but without teachers, meets at least once a month. All learners and teachers or researchers are involved in the plenary assembly. It meets only when convened by another committee, council or management.

5.10.5.1 Year group committee

Each year group holds a year group committee at least once a month. All learners who started school in the same year take part. All year group committees elect one learner each to the corridor service (executive), hear disputes in the education court (judiciary) and develop motions for the plenary assembly (legislation). As soon as there are urgent or sufficient motions for a plenary assembly, the year group committees agree on a date. The management, in voting with the teachers, can also call a plenary assembly.
The fixed groups, courses or classes always hold an additional course committee whenever there are concerns that only affect that group.

5.10.5.2 Plenary assembly

The plenary assembly is attended by all members of an educational institution. The year group committees collect motions that concern all learners of the educational institution and should become the rule. The teachers' council and council of managers also collect motions. The motions can consist of requests for what should be bought, what rules of conduct should apply, what excursions or projects should be offered and how the rooms should be used. At the plenary assembly, all motions are presented and voted on. At the plenary assembly, the leadership participates in order to be able to give information about feasibility and to raise objections if rules should violate the law.

5.10.6 Parents' council

In the nursery school and primary school there is also the parents' council, which sends a parent representative with speaking rights but without voting rights to the teachers' council and can also send them to the year group committee. The parents' council has a veto right over all decisions made in the year group and course committees. The parents' council makes its decisions with a majority of 65%.

5.10.7 Education court

The education court only meets when there has been a dispute that could not be settled or keeps recurring. All minors in out-of-home care have the right to bring the wrongdoer(s) before the education court if they feel they have been treated unfairly. Defendants can be children or teachers. Education courts take place within the framework of an extraordinary year group committee. Depending on which year group the affected person is in who files a charge, it is decided which year group committee is responsible. If the defendant is from a different year group, he or she is invited. The plaintiff and the defendant may each choose two learners as lawyers. The year group of the lawyer plays no role.

The year group committee meets and elects two voluntary learners as judges at the beginning. The plaintiff and defendant invite witnesses in voting with their lawyers. First the victim describes the course of events, then the offender, then the witnesses. Lawyers and judges can ask additional questions. Now the lawyers make pleas as to who is to blame for what. Afterwards, the two judges confer and announce what sentence is to be imposed. Violence, imprisonment or monetary payments are excluded. Specially devised sentences appropriate to the case or the current punitive measures are possible.

All present vote on whether this sentence is just. The teacher present has a right of appeal if a sentence is disproportionate or violates applicable laws. The sentence must then be revised by the judges in voting with the teacher present or the management. At the end of the court proceedings, a rule is established by all participants on how such misdeed can be prevented in the future. If such a rule already exists, this part is omitted and the sentence must be harsher. The corridor service makes sure that sentences are exported.

Should parents wish to appeal or convicted persons wish to lodge a revision, they must contact the responsible Municipal Court, which will then take over the case. Every sentence must be sent to the Education Authority and Youth Welfare Office.

5.10.8 Duty to inform

All meetings of councils, student councils, education courts and committees, form subgroups in the Education Directory on the group page of the educational institution. Minutes of the outcome of each meeting must be published there within 48 hours. Names are anonymised. A video recording must be made via the camera of a participant's People's Computer, which may only be interrupted when individual cases are discussed in which the names and offences of a person are in the foreground. The Education Authority and the Youth Welfare Office are given admission to all information without anonymisation, but are not allowed to publish it, only to use it for official purposes.

5.10.9 Educational policy content

Learners, teachers and researchers can make educational policy in their educational institution through the democratic structures and processes. For this purpose, the teachers' council works together with the student council and the committees. They decide independently who is hired as a new teacher, how rooms are occupied, how the grounds are used and what should be expanded or abolished.

5.10.9.1 Curriculum implementation

It is decided democratically what the curricula for the educational programmes in the subject areas will look like in order to achieve the Ministry of Education's target. The affected student council, together with the teachers of the subject, has the task of putting the curriculum into teaching forms through which the learners are able to pass the central performance records from the Ministry of Education. The teaching methods are adapted to the needs of the learners and their learning styles. Each student council and teacher has the right to make proposals for the content of the curriculum and for the way in which a performance record is to be delivered. These proposals are sent directly to the responsible teachers of the subject. Proposals for central performance records are sent to the Examinations Office. They are dealt with in the same way as a petition.[86]

5.10.9.2 Representation of interests

Learners can regularly express their interests in surveys or address them directly to the responsible teacher or student council. The student council is responsible for conducting the surveys and broadcasting them to the Institute of Education. If these are social interests that have nothing to do with the subject, the learner's wish or concern is brought to the upcoming committee that is responsible for it.

If a teacher requires a disproportionate amount of work compared to other courses, students should report this to their student council. The student council investigates the allegations by requiring teachers to disclose their past performance records such as tests, exams or assignments to the student council. If the allegations are confirmed, it will be an agenda item at the next meeting of the teachers' council. If the grievance is not resolved, the student council sends the

---

86 Ministry of State Organisation - 9.10.11.6 Petition

allegations to the Education Authority, which is obliged to clarify and invalidate the affected performance records.

5.10.9.3 Advice and complaints system

Every learner is informed of his/her rights at the beginning of a new school year in the first lesson. In college, this is done once during the induction session. The rights include admission to an advice and complaints system as well as to the democratic committees and student councils for learners.

The counselling centres consist of trained teachers who are employed as liaison teachers and school psychologists. The contact details of the liaison teacher or school psychologist are accessible via a notice with name, picture and contact details as well as on the school's profile page in the Education Directory. Complaints are received by the student council or, depending on responsibility, by the Education Authority or Examinations Office. Complaints can be noted in the surveys at the end of a school year or sent in person, by telephone, by post or by intranet during the school year. For this purpose, the Ministry of Education maintains links to the two sub-pages for "Advice" and "Complaints" on its intranet site. Each student council has a group in Education Directory through which those affected can contact them.

The Education or Examinations Office examines and deals with the complaints. If necessary, a representative of the office involved from the town hall responsible comes to the educational institution concerned to investigate complaints and hold discussions with all participants to clarify the case. The final report is sent to the personnel office in the Ministry of Education and to the management of the educational institution. The evaluation results must be discussed by the management with affected learners and teachers in person or in a committee.

If complaints and poor survey results are repeated 3 times, a warning is given to the responsible teacher. After a warning, the teacher can request a transfer. In case of a repeated offence, termination will follow.

5.10.9.4 Feedback round

If possible, a five-minute feedback session is held after each lesson or at least at the end of a lesson. There, learners say what they found good or bad. At least after the annual survey results have been sent to teachers by the Ministry of Education and published, there will be a one-hour feedback session in each course. Learners should write down their feedback, collect it and feed it into the surveys or feedback rounds.

5.11 Education tests

In order to increase learning success and to accompany the physical and mental development of minors, regular education tests are carried out. The tests are carried out at least at the beginning of the attendance in the nursery school, primary school, comprehensive school and college and stored in the learner's profile in the Education Directory. The affected learners and the responsible teachers have access to the results. Teachers can define specific learning methods for certain developmental levels, learning types or intelligence levels and include them in their duty roster so that learners can take them into account when compiling their timetable.

5.11.1 Developmental level test

The developmental stage test is a method for observation and documentary. It is currently available from Kuno Beller in his development table up to the age of ten.[87] It is continued until the age of majority and also includes the developmental areas of personality, sexuality and morality. The other developmental areas are fine motor skills, gross motor skills, cognition, language, play activity, social-emotional development, environmental awareness, body awareness and body care.
The test is continued annually and all results are continuously entered into the coordinate system and stored in the minor's

---

87https://www.beller-kkp.de/shop/de/entwicklungstabelle-
kinderentwicklung-kleinkindpaedagogik/kuno-bellers-
entwicklungstabelle-0-9

profile in the Education Directory. All teachers can access the entire history to adapt their teaching to the developmental level of the learners.

5.11.2 Learning type test

The learning type test enables learners and teachers to identify methods with which things can be learned faster and remembered longer. The learning types can be identified as a test, but rarely occur in pure form. Learning types are visual, auditory, motor or communicative. Learning types can change in the course of a lifetime or differ depending on the subject area, which rarely happens but is possible. Especially the phase of puberty makes changes possible. Therefore, learning type tests are conducted every time a student visits a new educational institution, then at least every 2 years and newly in each subject. All results are stored in the Education Directory and changes are shown to the learner. The result is announced to the teacher. In the Knowledge Directory, all contributions are keyworded according to learning types. There are different textbooks, teaching materials and methods for the different learning types.

5.11.3 IQ test

Every time a student changes or newly attends an educational institution, an intelligence quotient (IQ) test is conducted. This gives learners the opportunity to work on themselves or to be more patient with themselves. Teachers can adapt their language and lesson design to the intelligence level and form appropriate groups among learners. Every citizen has the right to take an IQ test at a state educational institution up to 4 times in his or her lifetime.

5.11.4 Results

The results are used for research purposes by the Ministry of Education. The aim is to research which learning methods lead to the greatest learning success at different IQ levels, learning types and developmental stages. The test results are compiled and evaluated by the Institute for Evaluation. The data will be cross-referenced with nursery school offerings and projects, types of lessons, performance records, final papers and grades from schools and colleges in order to identify successful learning opportunities and continuously develop them together with teachers.

5.12 Lesson planning

Lessons are designed differently at different educational institutions and adapted to age groups, learning types and subjects.

In the nursery school, offers and projects are taught in hybrid conceptions with group and theme rooms. Lessons are offered in small groups, the size of which is determined jointly by teachers and learners. In the primary school, lessons are held in the morning in compulsory subjects and classes, and in the afternoon in subject rooms, offers and projects that the children freely choose. In comprehensive school, there are compulsory subjects and electives that learners choose. In college, learners freely choose their course of study and then have to take compulsory courses and electives in that subject.

5.12.1 Hybrid concept

The hybrid concept extends from the nursery school to the college. It indicates how strongly learners and teachers are bound to each other. Open concepts give learners a lot of freedom of choice, provide little structure and allow free election of how, when and where learning takes place. Closed concepts give a fixed group in which learning takes place and everyone learns the same thing together at the same time. Which human prefers which concept is different and can vary according to subject, age or learning type. Roughly speaking, open concepts are more suitable for humans with a high willingness to learn and a disciplined life structure than closed concepts. Humans who do not have a good bond with family or friends and who are poor at self-motivation and organisation are more suited to a closed concept that gives them fellow humans, organisational structures and rewarding or punishing performance assessments. In the case of minors, teachers also involve parents; otherwise, the central performance records are used to measure performance. In the case of poor performance, the affected learner has a counselling session with the responsible teacher, the liaison teacher or the school psychologist to find the appropriate form of instruction.

5.12.1.1 Frontal teaching

The first type of teaching is classical frontal teaching, which is also called lecture in college. It is characterised by the presentation of texts, graphics, pictures, sound, video and illustrative material, moderated discussions and debates. The syllabus is arranged according to subjects and is worked through in a sequential manner. Lesson content is usually taught in a lecture, with the teacher speaking and the learners participating in the lesson by reporting and being called upon. Learning content is usually learned by heart in order to be able to apply it in performance records in tasks and to be able to rate the learning success.

5.12.1.2 Project teaching

The second type of teaching is project work. It is a mixture of frontal teaching and free learning. It is characterised by projects whose topics are determined jointly by the learners. In a large group, in small groups and individually, the course works to bring the project to a successful conclusion. The learners form groups independently. The teacher intervenes by drawing lots if no agreement can be reached. Those who want to change groups during group work phases must find swap partners. In the group work phases, group coordinators are elected secretly and directly by all group members. As soon as 50% of the group is dissatisfied with the work of a group coordinator, a new election takes place. Voluntary resignation is possible at any time, as is seeking exchange partners in the group. Individual work steps are determined and evaluated in voting. Lesson contents are alternately taught and practised. First, the theory is taught in a lecture, then groups work together to solve practical tasks, correct each other's completed tasks and present the results to a self-selected audience and the teacher for examination. Oral exams or presentations are graded. Projects are usually cross-curricular and deal with individual passages in the curriculum. The compilation of different projects, in which learners can choose to participate, makes it possible to cover the entire curriculum. Teachers with appropriate expertise support project groups, but are usually not experts themselves because the work is interdisciplinary. In a final presentation, the achievements of each individual project member are listed and the learning success is rated by expert teachers.

5.12.1.3 Free learning

The third type of teaching is free learning. It is characterised by tasks that teachers set for the learners, which they are supposed to complete in a given time. The learners themselves decide who does what, when and where. Learners primarily help themselves by posting their questions and requests for help on a blackboard or in the Education Directory. When posting, the task and its place in the syllabus must be indicated so that other year groups can also help. Those who post their request for help in the free learning group via the Education Directory can see learners who have achieved a good rating in the relevant performance record and are therefore particularly qualified as helpers. If no learner can be found as a helper, the teacher responsible for the respective subject must help. In this type of lesson, teachers are mainly involved in setting up tasks that reflect the curriculum and rating learners' completed tasks in order to measure learning. At the end of a lesson, learners who have had the same tasks must form two groups. Each group prepares a written or oral performance record for the other group, including a sample solution, which is controlled by the teacher and written by the other group. The group that created the performance record also corrects it. As with central performance records, the correction must be anonymous. The teacher checks the corrections and rates the performance records.

5.12.2 Selection and dial-up

The three types of teaching represent the hybrid concept. Learners are offered all types of teaching and can make their own choices. They are supported in their choice by the education tests. Teachers have to make notes when creating the lessons about which part of the lesson is suitable for which type of learner. When learners dial in at the beginning of a term, they can match this information with the results of their education tests and make choices more easily. Teachers may also have preferences for a particular type of teaching. They should indicate their preferences already in the lesson description in the duty roster. In principle, however, teachers are obliged to offer all types of lessons. The Education Authority makes sure that the demand for a particular type of teaching on the part of the learners is matched by a corresponding supply of teachers who are also happy to teach this type of teaching. Therefore, there may be transfers between year groups, subjects or educational institutions, which the Education Authority arranges in voting with the affected teacher and management.

5.12.3 Teaching materials

The Examinations Office provides handouts and copy templates for all three teaching methods. Those who develop their own teaching methods together with the learners should indicate this so that the learning success of the new method can be evaluated. Successful methods will be included in the handouts.

5.12.3.1 Practical examples

All teaching content must be transformed into practical examples by the Ministry of Education in cooperation with all appropriate ministries and voluntary companies. Practical examples always consist of the application of learning content from practical life. For example, the Ministry of Economy would have the third grade open and run a restaurant in the school cafeteria because it involves counting, weighing, adding, subtracting, multiplying and dividing various numbers. This simulation is accompanied by the teacher, who can demonstrate the work processes provided. The Ministry of Education can oblige companies in Planned Economy and Social Market Economy to publish their workflows for training purposes. If company secrets would be revealed, an older known production method must be used. The necessary theory is provided by the teachers, but the learners have to use it productively themselves. In project teaching, the theory is integrated into practice and can be used by the project participants independently and on their own responsibility to carry out the project. The final product and its presentation, including the process of creation, are graded. In addition, there is a cross-check test on the theoretical content.

5.12.4 Performance records

Teachers already indicate in the duty roster which form of performance record they would like to offer. In the first week, there is a voting with the present learners of the course. There is an election between exams, chores, oral exams or presentation exams. In order to enable a majority to participate in the course, the teacher must offer the performance record that the majority of the learners prefer. It is also possible that all forms of performance records are offered. For teachers, a low utilisation of their course due to an unpopular performance record would be dangerous. In the evaluation, it becomes apparent to the Education Authority that not many learners are being taught by the teacher, which can result in lower pay, a warning and also termination.

5.12.4.1 Failed central performance records

If learners fail a central performance record, they must repeat it if it is a compulsory subject. In the case of an elective subject, they can also choose another elective subject. It is not possible to skip individual examinations in an optional subject. If you want to complete an elective subject, you must pass all performance records in that subject. The completion of a certain number of electives is prescribed.

After the first failed attempt, the learner can seek support him/herself. On the second failed attempt, a counselling session with a competent teacher must take place and tutoring must be sought. On the third failed attempt, the lessons and the performance record must be repeated in frontal teaching. After the fourth failure, the underage learner must go to a boarding school in the Social Village or a special school until he/she has passed the performance record.

5.12.4.2 Digital performance records

Whether and how many performance records the teachers offer in the school year is up to them. It is permitted to produce an educational video on the topic as a performance record, which is graded. If more than one learner reports in the same subject in the same educational institution, the subject area is broadened. These videos are examined by the Examinations Office and published in the Knowledge Directory if they receive a good grade and are technically correct.[88]

The performance records can also be made on the computer, as a text file, questionnaire, presentation, video or as a real or virtual 3D model. There are special computer rooms, including a 3D printer. Before each performance record, there

---

88 Ministry of Media Affairs - 13.1 Cooperation with educational institutions, 13.2.1.1 News from research, 13.2.3.1 Textbook filming

is a system check against cheating software. The examinees are not allowed to bring anything to the examination except a drink and the clothes on their backs. The rooms are otherwise used for elaborate digital projects. All workstations have a mouse, keyboard and A4 graphic pad.

5.12.5 Question time

Before each performance record there is at least one question time where learners ask how a task works and other learners explain it. The teacher sits in and makes sure that everything is explained correctly. She also pays attention to how it was explained and whether more learners understood it as a result. If this is the case, they should document the explanation method together with this learner, try it out themselves and report it to the manager so that it can be shared in the Education Directory and used by other educational institutions through the council of managers.

5.13 Compulsory services

In the educational institutions, there are compulsory services, such as litter services, crossing guards, homework mentors, corridor services and tutoring. These services are provided by learners for learners to support each other. The rubbish service empties rubbish bins and collects carelessly discarded rubbish and tries to find the originators. Originators have to do additional litter duty. School crossing guards regulate traffic around educational institutions and provide increased safety at the beginning and end of school hours to prevent accidents between persons and vehicles. Homework mentors supervise younger learners if they have problems with their homework. Tutoring is provided by well graded learners for poorly graded learners. Compulsory services are distributed in the course committee or year group committee.

5.13.1 Corridor service

The corridor service consists of one learner per year group so that someone can always write and read the clock. In nursery schools, a teacher is involved for these two activities, who otherwise keeps a low profile. The corridor service is in contact with the management via radio. They ensure peaceful handling and a friendly tone, can settle disputes or call teachers for help. During breaks, the corridor service supervises the breaks, provides first aid in case of accidents and settles disputes or prevents students from hitting or annoying each other. Offences such as assault or insult are brought before the education court by the corridor service. The corridor service receives reports and also investigates offences itself on its rounds. If the offender and victim agree to settle their dispute themselves, the motto is "where there's no plaintiff, there's no judge". However, if the offender and victim are caught arguing 3 times in one month by the corridor service, the corridor service will take the case to the education court.

The apprentices in the corridor service change every month. Those who are not there on all days need a deputy. Each year group committee selects one learner each month for the coming weeks. The learner from the previous month becomes the deputy.

In the nursery school and primary school, the corridor service is also responsible for finding the children at the right time to go to an AG or to go home at a certain time.

5.13.2 Tutoring

Good learners help bad learners from a learning year lower. Good learners have grades 1 to 2, bad learners have grades 3 to 6. Tutoring is compulsory with grade 1 and from grade 4. These children have to stay longer after school and give or receive extra tuition. All courses are as similar in size as possible so that one-to-one support can be provided if necessary. If there is a shortage of tutors, learners with grades 1 to 2 can be called upon for tutoring. If this is also not sufficient, teachers are used. Tutoring is scheduled before homework and takes place directly after the end of lessons in free classrooms.

5.14 Holiday care

During the holidays, all educational institutions, except colleges, offer holiday care for minors. All premises are available for this purpose. Now is the time to carry out long-term offers and projects, such as building a ghost train, soapbox or hut. The staff of the nursery schools, afternoon care at primary schools and youth centres are responsible for the care. Participation is mixed-age. For example, kindergarten children can also attend holiday care at the comprehensive school, as long as they are no longer wearing nappies. 4 weeks before the holidays, all educational institutions must publish their holiday care programmes so that children can register for them up to 3 weeks before the holidays. The educational institutions should develop programmes with each other during the holidays and work together, for example in camps. It should be possible to alternate between the holiday care of several educational institutions and youth centres on a weekly basis. In youth centres, children and youths are given tasks that they can only manage in a team, the bigger the better. For example, building and designing meeting places or developing board games. These offers and projects can also be continued in the youth centre after the holidays.

5.15 Work and social behaviour

Teachers explain their working behaviour as a teacher and why they have the right to do this job on behalf of the people. They also explain their duty to supervise minors, which is assigned to them by their parents for the duration of the lessons.
The children should know that in the educational institution they learn knowledge that took mankind about 20 000 years to be able to do. The children learn this in only 12 years. Today, all humans in this country have this knowledge. For coexistence to work, you have to be able to do things at the beginning of life that you learn in educational institutions.

This explanation should be the justification for striving to learn. The more knowledge one has, the easier it is to live together because one can have more understanding for any circumstances.

Teachers pay attention to the behaviour of adolescents, which differs from that of adults and changes in several phases. Teachers have to accompany each of these phases and adapt the required work behaviour accordingly. The challenge is to facilitate the best possible development of each individual and at the same time not to cause damage to the community.

Teachers explain to the adolescents that work discipline is also taught in the educational institutions so that later colleagues can rely on each other at work. The head marks for work and social behaviour are the foretaste of later job references.

Each semester, head marks are awarded by all teachers who teach minors. The grading scale ranges from 1 for very good to 6 for unsatisfactory. The head grades for work and social behaviour result from all the following characteristics. They are collected in all educational institutions except colleges. Work behaviour includes precision, physical control and a sense of duty. Social behaviour includes willingness to learn, hierarchical awareness and the ability to work in a team.

5.15.1 Precision

Precise work behaviour is characterised by punctuality, diligence, promptness, cleanliness and correctness. Anyone who is prepared on time at the beginning of class by being at the workplace at the agreed time with all his or her working materials is considered punctual. Even those who do not complete their tasks quickly and correctly, but who try to work continuously and do not distract or allow themselves or others to be distracted, are considered diligent. Those who understand and execute tasks quickly are considered fast. He who forgets nothing and keeps his workplace clean is considered tidy. Whoever understands tasks correctly and solves them correctly or incorrectly, but after correction constantly solves them correctly, is considered correct.

5.15.2 Body control

As soon as the teacher enters the room, silence returns and everyone is in their places. No one speaks unless they have reported in advance and have been called by the teacher or the group coordinator. During lessons, there are periods of silence when full concentration is required.

5.15.3 Sense of duty

The tasks in class and the homework in the afternoon are to be completed independently, thoroughly, neatly and completely. Questions are permissible. If the subject matter is not understood, this must be reported to the teacher immediately. If the teacher sees the lack of understanding as a matter of practice, additional tasks must be completed for practice. If faults are found during the teacher's control of the assignments, these faults should be corrected by independent practice. Otherwise, poor marks in work behaviour and a parent interview will follow.

5.15.4 Willingness to learn

Every learner shows an attentive attitude to work, asks specific questions and reports immediately if something is not understood. This attention should be shown not only to the teacher, but also to all school staff, classmates and homework mentors or tutors.

5.15.5 Hierarchy awareness

Any explicit instructions given by the selected learners and the teachers must be followed. However, questioning of reasons is always allowed, as well as asking for the meaning and purpose of an instruction. Disparaging refutations or refusal to follow instructions will be punished.

Awareness should develop that someone rates the work, enforces order and has the right to do so because they act according to laws that are the will of the people. As long as learners abide by the rules, it will be a pleasant and interesting stay. In the case of misdeeds, sentences follow, just as imprisonment follows later in the case of criminal offences, and warnings follow in the case of misconduct on duty.

5.15.6 Ability to work in a team

The ability to work in a team is characterised by motivation, empathy, justice and courage. Those who can motivate themselves and others are considered motivated. Those who respect the feelings of others and help them to cope are considered empathetic. He who avoids injustice to himself and others and provides compensation and reconciliation is considered just. Those who take the first step, taking risks for the group and for the common good, are considered courageous. In an alliance of humans, the principle of solidarity prevails, which means that people help each other to abide by the rules. People bring it to the attention of their fellow human beings personally instead of telling on teachers. Tattling means reporting another person's offence to a supervisor without being personally affected. Instead, children should point out to each other when they commit wrongdoing. In case of doubt, the jurisprudence is taken over by the education court. Fellow children are neither teased nor beaten. Punitive measures are to be taken immediately when offences are committed. It is important to learn how conflicts can be solved through language and arguments rather than through violence.

In group work phases, group coordinators are always directly elected with a majority of at least 50% and re-elected from a deselection quorum of 50%. Group coordinators are allowed to reprimand lazy and unreliable group members and report them to the teacher in case of repeated offences. Depending on the frequency, punitive measures will follow.

5.16 Behavioural stages of adolescents

In nursery school, children have their autonomy phase, want to move a lot, explore everything and repeat things often. Teachers pay special attention to these needs by participating. During primary school, children are at the rule age, they still need a lot of movement, but they attach a lot of importance to rules and their observance, especially when it comes to fairness and equal treatment. Youths in comprehensive school are again in an autonomy phase where they need a lot of sleep, but also exercise. It is easy for them to unlearn things from primary school if they do not continue to practise them. They like to engage with the opposite sex and often develop feelings that favour love and affection. Disappointments, prohibitions and tabooing of these feelings generate hatred and envy. Teachers have the task of naming and explicitly praising love and affection through group therapy activities. In the case of disappointment, understanding must be ensured by asking disappointed ones and disappointing ones to name their feelings and how they got there, especially what circumstances led them to disappointing actions.

5.16.1 Mobbing

Bullying is a behaviour that mostly occurs among youths and can have an impact into adulthood. It has its origins in the developmental state of youths, who are particularly concerned with their self-worth during this phase. This is usually due to the fact that they are looking for partners for the first time because of sexual maturity or have a neglectful family. They are rated by humans and often rejected, even though they have loving feelings for that person. Comparisons with other persons who do or do not receive this love follow. Bullying usually serves to enhance one's own value by devaluing others. What already begins as annoyance in early childhood comes to a head in the course of sexual maturity when bullying takes place in a group. Many ally against one and the indifferent environment looks on idly or takes pleasure in it. The enjoyment is the basis for the upgrading of all participants and the devaluation of the bullied.

To prevent bullying before it occurs, teachers continuously educate pubescent adolescents about the physical and especially mental changes that are about to take place in their bodies.

If a case of bullying does occur, victims or observers can contact a teacher or any student council. Teachers and student councils have the duty to report a case of bullying to the management immediately.

Bullying is when someone is repeatedly annoyed by at least two persons within 2 weeks. Victims of bullying should record each offence by writing down the place, date, time, course of events, offender and witnesses.

Bullying is considered a criminal offence that must be tried in the education court because there are usually many participants involved, including failure to assist. The education court investigates the case and decides on the sentence. It sends its findings to the responsible school psychologist.

5.16.1.1 Criminal proceedings before the education court

The offences that the accused are always charged with in cases of bullying are insult or failure to render assistance. There may also be more serious charges, such as assault, coercion, stalking or worse. If serious charges are brought and supported by evidence, a report is made to the local Municipal Court.

Before the education court, all those affected are heard and a verdict is reached on the question of guilt and the sentence. Due to bias, all affected year groups may be excluded from the election of the judge and the voting on the sentence. However, the roles of witnesses and lawyers may also be played by biased persons who are not themselves defendants. All punitive measures of the educational institutions are open to the education court as sentences. The harshest possible sentence is the upbringing camp.

5.16.1.2 Psychological reappraisal

In cases of bullying, the management contacts the school psychologist and makes an appointment, which takes place after the educational court proceedings. A specially trained educational psychologist travels to the educational institution and has all participants meet for group discussions. The first group discussion lasts about 45 minutes. Offenders and victims are clearly identified. Why is the person being bullied? Who is bullying and how? Why are the others only watching and not intervening? As homework, the accused should write at least 2 pages on why they acted the way they did, what their motives were, where the motivation came from, why they want to upgrade themselves, who devalued them or devalued them once in their life and how. A responsible teacher collects the homework the next day and sends it to the school psychologist. Those who do not have this homework receive a punitive measure from the teacher.

After the initial group discussion, the victim and main offender are asked to attend a one-to-one interview with the school psychologist lasting about 20 minutes, where individual appointments can also be made with psychologists in private practice.

The day after next follows the second group discussion between the school psychologist, offender and victim. The school psychologist evaluates the homework in order to invite all participants involved in his opinion. At the beginning, both sides read out their homework. Now the enemies are to tell each other why they don't like each other and what they see as a bad quality or habit about each other. Then they are to say how this could be improved, i.e. what behaviour of the other could make them friends. This group discussion lasts about 45 minutes. After four weeks, the visit of the school psychologist is investigated in a survey by the learners. The questionnaire should state whether one was an offender, victim or bystander and what has changed since then. This survey is sent to the responsible school psychologist who can repeat the procedure or take other measures if necessary.

5.17 Punitive measures

Punitive measures only apply to minors, but can still be implemented for poor work and social behaviour. Poor work and social behaviour of adults results in teachers starting to apply head marks to learners of age of majority.

There are light and heavy punitive measures. The light punitive measures are punitive work, detention in school and parent talks. The severe punitive measures are monetary fines, expulsion from school, expulsion from school, upbringing camp or special school. All offences result in an entry in the school record on the learner's profile in the Education Directory. Minor offences are punished with minor penalties, but if they accumulate, they are followed by a severe penalty. Severe penalties also follow serious offences.

For all punitive measures ordered by a teacher, the course committee has the right of veto in the first instance, the year group committee in the second instance, the plenary assembly in the third instance and the management in the last instance. The veto is deemed to be fulfilled as soon as 60% of the course, year group or educational institution cast their vote in the veto quorum on the respective group page in the Education Directory. The educational institution manager can veto at any time. If the veto is used, an education court will be convened immediately.

5.17.1 Penalty work

In the nursery school, it is necessary to do clean-up work for others as punishment work. During the punishment work, a teacher is supposed to talk to the child about the offence and find out why the child did it. A record of the outcome of the discussion is placed in the school file in the Education Directory. From primary school onwards, the punishment work consists of two parts. In the first part, you have to write why you did the offence. Depending on the age, the amount of text required increases. The first part is for the learner's self-reflection. In the second part, you have to do a task that the teacher chooses from the following. Either one does an additional homework in the subject in which one is worst or one does a lesson protocol.

5.17.1.1 Lesson protocol

A lesson protocol where you are allowed to stay in the room must be a progress report. All comments and explanations should be recorded as verbatim as possible. For this purpose, the teacher activates a sound recorder that is connected to a voice recognition software and directly records everything that is said. The lesson protocol is then compared, graded and included in the overall grade.

A lesson protocol where you have to go out the door has to become a results protocol. Here, the offender is dependent on his classmates who can, but do not have to, inform him of the results. This lesson protocol is also graded and is included in the overall grade.

5.17.2 Detention in school

Detention in school occurs when a learner fails to complete a task in class. This detention in school lasts only until the task is completed. Detention in school as a sentence for an offence is always associated with an exercise that is poorly mastered and of which there is constant repetition. This can range from sitting still, to copying a text, to writing a performance record. The duration of detention in school increases with age.

5.17.3 Parents' meeting

If there are 10 or more punitive measures, there will be a parent interview with the teacher and if there are 20 punitive measures, there will be a parent interview with the teacher and the head. Parent interviews due to poor work and social behaviour are chargeable. They are calculated from the hourly wage of the teacher and, if applicable, also of the head, multiplied by the time required for preparation, implementation and follow-up of the parent interview. A parent interview due to poor grades in individual subjects is free of charge.

5.17.4 Monetary fine

For each entry of a penalty in the school record, a fee is due which is equal to the hourly wage of the teacher and, if applicable, the management, multiplied by the time spent plus a 10% profit mark-up. The monetary fine is due at the end of a semester. The punitive measures upbringing camp and special school are chargeable and must be worked off by detention by a parent if necessary.

5.17.5 School exclusion

Expulsion means that a learner is not allowed to attend the educational institution for 2 weeks. Thus, exclusion from school is equivalent to an immediate expulsion and a temporary ban from the building. A school exclusion can only take place once at an educational institution, the second time a school expulsion must take place.

5.17.6 Expulsion from school

Expulsion from school means that one has to change educational institutions. Before being allowed to attend another educational institution, one has to go to the upbringing camp for 3 months, which is only possible once during the primary school years. Expulsion from school can also mean that one has to attend the special school until one's grades in work and social behaviour are below 4.0 on average. If the management offers both options, the learner has the election.

5.17.7 Upbringing camps

After 40 entries in the school record, a grade point average of more than 4.0 in both head grades, expulsion from school or a serious offence according to the judgement of the education court, minors are sent to the upbringing camp for 3 months and one parent is liable to detention for one week. If the head marks remain above the average of 4.0, the student must transfer to a special school.

Only children between the ages of 4 and 18 are admitted to the upbringing camp. Upbringing camps take place in a Social Village and are run according to need. The stay of minors is never longer than 3 months. The daily schedule corresponds to the basic training curriculum of the German Armed Forces in 2002, with the exception of military tactical instruction and shooting training. In their place, the current curriculum is taught in frontal teaching. Here, it is more about practising good work and social behaviour and punishing violations instead of working through the educational content of the curriculum. For example, if someone talks without being asked or called on, the whole class has to walk a lap around the upbringing camp. Missed classwork, must be done after dinner or on the weekend. As a substitute for the time on the shooting range, individual or group therapy sessions are held. On weekends, participants are not allowed to go home, but must work through cleaning tasks in the buildings and on the grounds.

6 Special school[89]

Special schools are opened by the Ministry of Education when there is sufficient need. They are always established in the educational centres of the Social Villages. All minors who have problems with work and social behaviour, are at risk of not being able to complete their comprehensive schooling or are highly gifted go to the special school. A special school always specialises in one of these three characteristics.

The special school is a combination of primary school and comprehensive school with the same forms of teaching as in other educational institutions, except that there are twice as many teachers per pupil and additional educationalists, psychologists and sports, music and drama therapists. Individual tuition is possible at times because there are always two teachers per course. In cases of hardship, permanent one-to-one care can be approved or boarding can be prescribed.

89 §177.6 School system: BV Art. 62

Because each special school is located in a Social Village, minors can live in the children's home outside school hours. Then the special school becomes a boarding school, which can be used temporarily or permanently until school graduation.

6.1 Special school for the behaviourally disturbed

Minors must attend the special school if they have already been to the upbringing camp 2 times and their grades in work and social behaviour are below 4.0 on average.

The students live in a boarding school with a strict daily routine and lots of sports throughout the day. In the mornings there are classes and in the afternoons individual counselling therapies by psychologists alternate with sports, music and theatre therapies in the group. Those who refuse to participate have to stay in their rooms. Students are only allowed to go home at weekends and only if they are on good behaviour. On weekends, there are therapies in the morning, sports in the afternoon and performances of the theatre, film, music, art and sports groups in the evening. As soon as the head marks have reached an average of 2.0 and there are no punitive measures in the school year, the special school may be left again.

6.2 Special school for the learning disabled

Minors must attend the special school if they have a grade point average of over 4.0 in the school subjects but not in the head grades and are already one year behind in the curriculum. As soon as the grade point average of 2.0 is achieved and the delay has been made up, the children can attend the usual educational institutions again. If the grade point average does not improve, an attempt should be made to achieve the basic qualification by the age of majority. All children who attend the special school because of learning disabilities do not have to live in the children's home, but are allowed to return home after completing their compulsory education. However, if the parental residence is too far away, they cannot commute.

6.3 Special school for the gifted

This type of special school does not count as a punitive measure. Minors can attend the special school if they are highly gifted. They are prepared as quickly as possible to take the college entrance qualification in order to be able to start studying at a college. These minors can also live in the children's home, but they do not have to.

7 Nursery school

The Ministry of Education operates nursery schools for early education for children from the age of 2 to 6. Attendance at the nursery school is not compulsory, but can become compulsory from the age of four if the preschool test is not passed. A curriculum applies in all these nursery schools, as in all other educational institutions. In curriculum development, economic stakeholders are replaced 50% by primary school teachers to ensure a seamless transition.

Teachers who have completed a course of study to become a teacher specialising in social education are employed to provide education and care for the children. They are called educators and addressed by their first names. In voting with the surrounding primary school, teachers from the primary school are used for pre-school education in the nursery school and, vice versa, educators from the nursery school are used for afternoon care in the primary school. At least 2 educators of a nursery school must be male or female so that children can get to know both genders and learn about bonding. For quality development, procedures for observation and documentation are used, which are the central performance records in the nursery school. On the one hand, these procedures serve the children and parents to know what stage of development they are in. On the other hand, they serve educators to develop suitable offers and projects. In addition, the data is sent to the Institute of Education for research on human early childhood education and development.

Once a year, an employee of the Youth Welfare Office comes unannounced to each nursery school and checks the conditions. Another time he comes announced and informs the children about their rights. He informs the children that they can turn to him in all matters of parenting and development and where they can reach him at what times and at what address or telephone number. A direct voice connection between the Youth Welfare Office and the child in the nursery school is established via the device for the child emergency call[90] . A device for the child emergency call with intercom function must be placed in all nursery schools near the floor in a place accessible to the children.

7.1 Concept

Each nursery school writes its own concept in which they describe their premises, equipment, educators' skills, local conditions and their parenting style. The conception must be adaptable to the children who live with it. The concepts correspond in part to those of Froebel[91] , Montessori[92] , Reggio[93] , Neil[94] and Waldorf education[95] . Basically, there is the open and closed concept in every nursery school, which is why it is called a hybrid concept. Children should decide for themselves whether they want to grow up in an open or closed concept.

In an open concept, the children can decide for themselves with whom they want to go to which thematic room and when, what they want to occupy themselves with or in which offer or project they want to participate. This concept is suitable for children who want to be independent.

Other children would rather have the same humans around them on a regular basis, do things together and have fixed daily structures. Children also switch between these two preferences. Therefore, it should be possible for them to change to a fixed group, i.e. a closed concept, every 6 months. The exit is possible at any time, but then for at least 6 months.

90 Ministry of Family Affairs - 8.2 Children's Emergency Hotline
91 https://www.friedrich-froebel-online.de/
92 http://www.montessori.de/
93 https://www.kindergartenpaedagogik.de/1138.html
94 https://www.kinderpolitik.de/datenschutz/20-kinderrechte/
wegbereiterinnen-und-wegbereiter/60-alexander-sutherland-neill
95 https://www.kindergartenpaedagogik.de/2203.html

In order to be able to create a sense of community and solidarity even in the open concept, there are the regular year group committees, which can also decide on joint excursions or projects. Every educational institution should be adaptable enough to be able to implement both concepts, i.e. to open or dissolve fixed groups. The decision for a fixed group or its dissolution must be decided by a majority in a plenary assembly and documented by video.

7.2 Building & outdoor area

The building and its equipment are aligned with the curriculum and child development. The following use of space is exemplary of how the educational areas can be covered.

The multi-purpose room is soundproofed, has a stage and can be darkened. Children can sleep in it when they are tired. It is important for children to be able to sleep when they are tired. Stackable and adjustable-size cots can be placed in the multi-purpose room. The beds can be pulled apart telescopically and the slatted grid unfolds in a diamond shape to become increasingly coarse-meshed. The mattresses are made of washable foam and can be extended by rectangular foam pieces. Blankets, playbacks for audio games or music boxes in cuddly toys can be taken from the relaxation room. Theatre can be played with role-play costumes to embody social, unpopular or popular roles.

A variety of board and card games are available in the games and dining room. Snacks are available for children at the self-service counter outside meal times.

In the construction room, all kinds of materials such as cuddly toys, dolls, doll's houses, building blocks, Duplo, Lego, Playmobil or Knex can be used to build landscapes and re-enact situations. As a digital supplement, 3D models, drawings and films can be made on computers.

The craft room offers many materials, paints and design tools to create works of art or utilitarian objects or toys. The consumables consist of non-hazardous waste to practice the circular economy. In the laboratory, biological, chemical and physical experiments can be done and one's own body or the environment can be explored. Craftsmanship is required in the workshop when tools and machines are used to shape wood, plastic, metal and fabric.

In the relaxation room, the children can relax on a sofa, listen to music and audio books via headphones or read books. Dream journeys, mandalas and chi gong exercise sessions invite you to linger.

In the group room, children can become part of a fixed group on a voluntary basis and have their strengths specifically strengthened and their weaknesses weakened by their caregivers. Therefore, this room with direct connection to the outdoor area offers something from all other rooms.

There is at least one outdoor area per nursery school with grass, beds, sand, paving stones and soft ground under climbing facilities. There are also poles to hang waterproof awnings by zip and snap hooks as a canopy. In the outdoor area there is either at least one tree to climb or a climbing frame. In the sandbox there is a digger frame and next to the sandbox a rotating water pump with pump lever, which can be swivelled either via a drain in the ground or via a water feature with drainage channels and at least one water wheel. At least one fruit or nut tree grows on the outdoor area and the bed has at least one greenhouse. The lawn can be equipped with goals.

7.3 Equipment for children

Every nursery school has clothing storage facilities where parents can drop off or lend out clothing that has become too small for their children aged between 0 and 5 years. All parents are allowed to lend out clothes there until their children are too big for them. The rule is that clothes are always returned to the place where they were lent out. Destroyed or missing clothes only have to be replaced if there is still enough space in the camp. The same applies to children's seats, prams or similar equipment. Every item in storage is photographed and published in the swap shop on the nursery school's group page in the Education Directory and sorted by educational institution. There, parents and children can choose things they want to lend out and until when. On the page of a part it says in which nursery school it is located and whether it can only be picked up or also sent. Items that have been borrowed are also displayed, as well as the date on which they will be returned. Anyone who has lent something out receives a list in which all their loans are recorded. The list is displayed in the person's own profile in the Education Directory.

7.4 Special nursery school

In the special nursery school, children aged 0 to 6 are cared for around the clock, seven days a week. Parents who would have to leave their children alone due to shift work or urgent appointments may drop off their children at the special day care centre or make use of the pick-up and drop-off service for which a fee is charged. The costs are settled via the child benefit. These special nursery schools exist in every Social Village as a cooperative venture between the nursery school in the Education Centre and the children's home[96] .

In the special nursery school, children who are difficult to raise as well as physically and mentally handicapped children up to primary school age are also cared for. The staffing ratio here per child is at least twice as high as in other nursery schools. Specially trained staff for disabled children and children with behavioural problems look after these children in small groups.

7.5 Voluntary nursery school

Families can set up a unification and create a profile for a voluntary nursery school in the Labour Directory. At the same time, they automatically open a group in the Education Directory. One parent supervises up to 4 children and receives the hourly rate of child benefit per child. Each family can register as a service provider or consumer via the nursery school's profile. Voluntary nursery schools are regularly inspected by the Youth Welfare Office[97] and receive a seal of approval including assessment and grade, which must

96 Ministry of Planned Economy - 18.1.7 Children's House, 18.1.8 Education Centre
97 Ministry of Family Affairs - 7.6 Youth Welfare Office

be published on the homepage of their profile and on the entrance door.

7.6 Infant care

Infants aged 0 to 2 years should be able to be at home with their parents. Therefore, attendance at a state nursery school is only possible from the second year of life. However, if parents do not want this, there are crèches where children can be taken while they are still breastfeeding. For round-the-clock care, children can be taken to the nearest special nursery school.

7.6.1 Crèche

The crèche is attended by infants aged 0 to 2 years. In voting with the municipal population, a state nursery school may also include a crèche. It is forbidden to run crèches alone, in order to avoid a change of caregivers at this early stage of life. In this phase of life, one educator is responsible for 5 infants at a time. The way of working is similar to Emmi Pikler's concept.[98] Here, it is particularly important to ensure that the infant has more good than bad experiences in its life in order to be able to develop a basic trust. Since hearing is already developed in the womb, children understand much more than they can express. Therefore, as long as they are not yet able to walk, toddlers should be moved around in their arms or in a pram so that, over time, they can be shown all the details and called by name. Educators set up a course by distributing everyday objects around the room or garden. All the children are allowed to join in and say to the toddlers what the thing in front of them is called and what it can do. Since children can make gestures rather than sounds at the beginning of their lives, the educators speak to them in signs and spoken language. The aim is to give children with little motor skills the opportunity to communicate at an early age.

98https://www.kindererziehung.com/Paedagogik/Alternative-Erziehung/Pikler-Paedagogik.php

7.7 Observation and documentary

Educators have two forms of observation for their performance records. Both forms of observation complement each other to form a profile of strengths and weaknesses. Data entry is done digitally via standardised observation sheets that are made available to the children in their profile in the Education Directory. All data collected in the nursery school belongs to the child and is administered by his or her legal guardians. The nursery school, the Youth Welfare Office and the Institute for Education are allowed to collect and use the data, but have a duty of confidentiality towards third parties.

The first form of observation is developmental observation and corresponds to quantitative social research. It serves to classify each child in physical, emotional and mental developmental stages. This makes it possible to form groups among the children so that the necessary educational experiences can be made to master all developmental stages. The instruments are scientifically tested on an ongoing basis and are comparable to Kuno Beller's development table.[99] The Institute for Education is responsible for the development and distribution to the educators.

The second form of observation is educational observation and corresponds to qualitative social research. It is based on recording and documenting each child's strengths and special features. Comparisons with other children are avoided. In portfolios, the children collect all their strengths and special features, which can be documented using various media. Children are given the opportunity to discover their natural talents. Instruments that have been scientifically tested are the Leuven Engagement Scale[100] and the Education and Learning Stories from the German Youth Institute[101] .

This data is entered in the child's profile in the Education Directory via the People's Computer of the respective educator and is only stored there. This means that parents and children

99 https://www.beller-fortbildung.de/konzept-kuno-beller-entwicklungstabelle.html
100 http://www.leuvener-engagiertheitsskala.de/
101 https://www.dji.de/ueber-uns/projekte/projekte/bildungs-und-lerngeschichten-im-elementarbereich.html

can see at any time which data the educator has recorded and when it is accessed and by whom. This enables educators to develop suitable offers and projects for individual or several children with the same strengths or weaknesses.

7.7.1 Education and research

There are educators working in nursery schools who are involved in research just like all other teachers. They conduct ongoing studies on early childhood development, family structures, socialisation, resilience and successful learning models and learning tools. The studies are led by the affected state colleges and the Institute of Education.

7.8 Support areas

The support areas in the nursery school include subject areas that are reflected in the rooms and their equipment. The time in the nursery school should be used to gain initial non-binding experience with as many subject areas as possible. Therefore, the educators offer educational opportunities in the following areas: Emotionality, Social Relationships, Health, Hygiene, Movement, Nutrition, Clothing, Life Practices, Language, Writing, Media, Music, Dance, Mathematics, Science, Technology, Ethics, Democracy, Politics, Society, Environment, Economy, Culture, Visual and Performing Arts.[102] Some of these educational opportunities are present in every child's everyday life, such as democracy, ethics, politics and society in the councils and committees. Other subjects are available for the children to choose from.

For the phase when children continuously ask "Why?", there is a Tablet PC that can be used to watch videos from the Knowledge Directory. If an explanation does not yet exist, the child can speak the question into the camera and microphone of the Tablet PC. The video is published in the Knowledge Directory and users can create answer videos that are stored under the question in the Knowledge Directory.

---

102 https://bep.hessen.de/sites/bep.hessen.de/files/BEP_2019_Web.pdf

7.8.1 Goals and examinations

The aim is to make technical achievements of mankind tangible in a playful way. In every nursery school there are tests once a year that the children have to pass. However, these tests should not be labelled as such, but are wrapped up in a game or simply observed and recorded. Children with abnormalities are first reported to their parents; if nothing improves, the supervising teachers should inform the Youth Welfare Office so that the Youth Welfare Office can help with family counsellors and issue sentences against the parents if they refuse.

In the first year of life, the child should be able to crawl, laugh or cry. In the second year of life, the child should be able to walk or talk, in the third year to walk and talk. In the fourth year of life, the child should be able to run through a course and say a sentence without mistakes. The course covers spatial orientation, such as right, left, front and back. After a child has run-through the course, he/she should guide another child through the course by voice commands. In the fifth year of life, the final test is taken. The course is extended and repeated, but blindfolded and with a pilot. Now, in addition to movement, things have to be felt, smelled, tasted and named blindfolded. A story is to be retold, as well as a common experience that already happened at least 3 days ago. As the last part of the final exam, a child has to show the educator his or her own project, such as a building made of sand or building blocks, or create another project result in a group. All exams are videotaped by an educator showing the child completing the exam. The video must be taken with a People's Computer and saved in the child's profile in the Education Directory.

7.8.2 Pre-school test

All four-year-olds must take the preschool test at the local state nursery school. This test lasts one week, during which the child attends the nursery school during opening hours for at least 6 hours a day. Educators observe whether the child is able to run-through a course to the right, left, front and back, as well as say a sentence without mistakes and do a retelling of the past meal. Over the course of the week, the educators observe whether the child is able to control his or her body, eat food, put on and take off clothes, keep to the toilet, play alone and with other children, be tense and relaxed. If the child does not reach the learning goals, he/she must attend preschool care until he/she masters them. Pre-school care ensures that school readiness is achieved by the time compulsory schooling begins at age 6. For this purpose, the pre-school test is compulsory. If enrolment in school under these circumstances would overburden a child too much, preschool compulsory care exists in the 5th year of life.

8 Primary school

The Ministry of Education runs primary schools, which have fewer pupils than comprehensive schools and are also found in smaller towns. Children usually attend primary school from the age of 6 to 10. Exceptions apply when children repeat or skip classes. Learners are grouped by class and receive instruction in all primary school subjects as a class community. Primary school teachers are called teachers and addressed by their last name. The children are told that this type of school was almost always used in the past. With this type of school, they get to know a way of imparting knowledge in rigid structures, such as classes, fixed teachers and timetables.

The primary school period falls within the rule age of the children and is used to prepare the children for the independent preparation of a timetable in the comprehensive school. The timetables are predetermined, as are the teachers. The only possibility of exerting influence remains the veto quorum against teachers' decisions and their voting by a committee.

Everyday life in the primary school is clearly regulated. Before school starts, children are allowed to play in the playground. The school bell rings three times, then all pupils must line up in rows of two according to class. The teachers of the first lesson call their classes into the classroom. There is silence in a row of two, but gestures may be used to communicate. Depending on whether the children stay until noon or in the evening, the primary school changes. Compulsory lessons take place mainly in the morning. Strict adherence to the rules and implementation of the curriculum are enforced, if necessary with punitive measures such as bad grades, detention in school or punitive work. Afterwards, the children can go home or to afternoon care. While work life is simulated in the morning, family life is simulated in the afternoon. The children can choose the form of care in fixed groups or freely in themed rooms. They get lunch and dinner and can use all the rooms of the primary school. Educators from the surrounding nursery schools look after the children in cooperation with the primary school teachers. In special primary schools in the Social Villages, there is also an extended care offer for overnight stays or at the weekend.

The aim of primary school is firstly to teach basic knowledge such as reading, arithmetic, writing, paying attention, being polite, creative and independent. Secondly, the primary school period should be used to discover talents in each child and to promote them so that they can be followed up with suitable elective subjects in the comprehensive school.

8.1 Form of teaching

Before enrolment and at the beginning of a school year, education tests are conducted to sort the pupils into their classes. In the case of developmental levels and IQ, the children with the similar level are schooled together in order to be able to promote and address them specifically. The learning type decides whether they attend a class with project teaching, frontal teaching or free learning. Teachers decide with which form of instruction they can best convey the learning content. If they notice that a child could learn better with another teacher using a different teaching method, they can refer the child there. The referral is agreed with the child and can be done on a trial basis, by the hour, by subject or with a change of class.

8.2 Change of school

Primary schools have a catchment area. All children of compulsory school age and learners living within the primary school's catchment area attend a primary school until it is at capacity. Those who move can change primary schools. Pupils may apply to the head teacher for a maximum of one voluntary change of primary school. Punitive measures can trigger a pupil's expulsion from school and force parents to change schools.

8.3 Seating arrangement

In primary school, the teacher determines the seating arrangement by placing the desks in an appropriate order. He can transfer pupils as a punitive measure, but for a maximum of 6 months. Pupils hold an election to determine their seat neighbour. At the beginning of each school year, each pupil is asked to write 4 names for his or her right and left seat neighbour on a piece of paper. To do this, all students sit in a circle and place numbers in front of them in ascending numerical order. The teacher has a class list with the names and behind it are the numbers for each name. All pupils write up to 4 numbers on a piece of paper. Those who do not care who they sit next to do not write down a number. If you really want a certain pupil to sit next to you, write down only that number. If you write down 4 numbers, you will definitely get one of these students as your seatmate. Teachers collect all the slips of paper, enter the results in the list and automatically receive lists of who wanted whom. These results are handed out to the students individually and everyone has to personally choose 2 from all their applicants.

8.4 Special primary school

Every primary school in a Social Village is also a special primary school. The overnight stays take place in the children's house. This primary school offers flexible teaching times, a transport service and overnight accommodation. Shift workers have the option of having their children schooled from 8 am to 12 pm or 1 pm to 5 pm. A weekly change is also possible. For children whose parents work at night, there is a transport service that picks them up from their local primary school and takes them to the special primary school. If it is a weekday, the child can also be dropped off again at the local primary school by the transport service the next morning. On Fridays, the child can stay over the weekend. Parents can pick up their child themselves or use the transport service. If parents are away on business, the child can stay at the special primary school for that long. The services of the special primary school are settled via the child benefit.

8.5 Knowledge transfer

Primary school pupils use the People's Computer exclusively at school, rarely in class and mostly in committees. From the age of 10, it is theirs and they are allowed to take it home.

In the primary school, screens are predominantly dispensed with when imparting knowledge. The primary school is designed to be as free as possible from digital technology. The learning processes according to human evolution are to be emulated. Clear production processes with paper and pencil in craftsperson work, with chalk on the blackboard that can be folded open and closed and must be cleaned.

No matter what knowledge is to be imparted, an example is shown first, which can be executed by the learners themselves after the learning process. For example, a text is read aloud that the children can read aloud themselves after one month. Whenever possible, knowledge should be told when it was invented. For example, the "+" sign was introduced in 1489. Today's practical application of knowledge in different areas is presented to the learners. For example, mental arithmetic must be used when shopping. Only in the following step is the knowledge explained and practised. For example, that 2 + 8 = 10 and the "+" sign here can be considered like an "and". In order to learn to calculate in the tens space, learners in a class set each other arithmetic problems with their fingers. Learned knowledge is always applied practically by the learners. For example, children are asked to build a shop and equip it with empty packaging in order to practise arithmetic. In the last step of knowledge transfer, knowledge is passed on to other learners. Learners should not replace teachers. Learners who did not understand the teacher's first explanation should have the topic explained to them in the presence of the teacher in the language of a peer. The teacher just makes sure that nothing is explained incorrectly. For example, this learning method can be used in a question time or with homework mentors.

The tasks should be linked to fun. For example, a word puzzle makes a funny sentence or a maths problem is part of a funny story. Pupils should know from the beginning what they are supposed to learn knowledge for and how they can use it for their personal benefit. Especially in primary school, there are many areas that stimulate children's imagination. For example, maths is inextricably linked to physics and physics deals with space, which fascinates children.

8.6 Grading

Grades for performance records in the primary school are only awarded to the Examinations Office, the Headmaster and, at the request of the pupils, also to them personally or also to their parents. If a warning or demotion in a subject or transfer to a lower class level has been noted in the half-year report, parents always receive a testimonial. Grades are used for rating learners, teachers and skipping a grade. Otherwise, there is always only the indication "Pass" or "Fail". Grades 1 to 4, for example, are considered to be a pass and 5 to 6 are considered to be a fail. In the case of a grade 1, the teacher can praise the child and have him/her explain to the class how he/she learned and how he/she went about solving the problem. The aim is for primary school pupils to learn to share the best strategies so that everyone can benefit. From a grade of 1, a pupil can go to the next higher class in a subject. With a grade point average of 1.2, a student can skip a grade.

8.6.1 Transfer[103]

Transfer means promotion to a next higher class level. If too many tasks are not passed, this can result in a downgrade, which means that one is not transferred to the next higher class level. The school subjects in which reading, writing and arithmetic are learned are decisive, which is why they are called main subjects.

After the first grade, one is not transferred if one still does not pass the preschool test despite preschool. In the second grade, one may not have a 6 in a major subject and a 5 in all major subjects. In the third grade, you may not have a 5 in any major subject and a 4 in all major subjects. In the fourth grade, the grade point average may not exceed 4.0, with the main subjects counting double.

Downgrades in primary school result in compulsory afternoon care with tutoring and additional tasks. Those who are two times not transferred in the primary school must attend the special school.

The comprehensive schools provide the primary schools with the knowledge that primary school pupils must have in order to be able to transfer to the comprehensive school. The primary school certificate with which the fourth grade has been successfully completed is regarded as the qualification.

---

103 §176.4 Education space

8.7 Timetable

Class	1	2	3	4
Age	6 to 7	7 to 8	8 to 9	9 to 10
Teaching content	National language, maths, art, music, ethics, handicrafts, writing and design, sport	National language, maths, art, music, ethics, handicrafts, writing and design, sport	National language, Maths, Art, Music, Ethics, Homeland and subject lessons, Textiles, Writing and design, Sport	National language, Maths, Art, Music, Sex education, People's Computer, Textiles, Crafts, Sport

8.7.1 Times

The timetable provides the daily schedule, which the educational institutions can adapt to their local needs. In the alliance between several primary schools and at least one special primary school, all points of the daily schedule are to be offered.

7:00 – 7:55 Breakfast buffet
Compulsory lessons start
    8:00 – 8:45 hour1
    8:50 – 9:35 hour2
    9:35 – 10:00 Yard break1
    10:00 – 10:45 hour3
    10:50 – 11:35 hour4
    11:35 – 12:00 Yard break2
    12:00 – 12:45 hour5
Compulsory lessons end
    12:45 – 13:45 Lunch
    13:45 – 14:00 Exercise break
    14:00 – 15:00 Homework and exercises

15:00 – 18:00 Playing or sports and music through
clubs
18:00 – 19:00 Dinner
19:00 – 20:00 Playing or sport and music through
clubs
20:00 – 20:30 Transfer to the special primary school
20:30 – 21:00 Reading aloud, listening to radio plays,
reading
21:00 – 22:00 Get ready for bed and go to sleep

8.7.2 Breaks

During the breaks, music is played in at least one room or on part of the schoolyard so that the children can dance. The third and fourth classes run the school radio. The school radio plays music from the wish list, which is displayed on the notice board and where you can write a song or add your name to an existing song.

8.7.3 Rubbish

Children are made aware that it is a criminal offence to dispose of litter in nature.[104] There are litter officers in the classes who take care of littering and emptying the dustbins in the classroom. Students are assigned in turn to collect rubbish on the school grounds during breaks. On all excursions, there are litter officers who take a pair of tongs and a litter bag, collect litter and make sure that the other children put their litter back in the bag, dispose of it with them or in a litter bin.

8.7.4 Subjects

The subjects and their contents correspond to the curriculum. They are offered in the respective primary schools with suitable teaching methods as frontal teaching, project or free learning.

---

104 Ministry of Justice - 8.6.1 Environmental pollution

8.7.4.1 National language

In the national language lessons, everything is taught to be able to deal with the domestic language. Reading is started with. The alphabet, the pronunciation of the letters and their combinations are read and sung. Words are read out by the teacher or able pupils and repeated by the whole class. The same follows later for sentences and stories.

Writing is learned by copying. The alphabet is to be copied 1000 times in upper and lower case letters, whereby only 500 times the alphabet is written, followed by 500 repetitions of a pair of letters (Aa, Bb, etc.) until it is the turn of the next pair of letters of the alphabet. Words follow, sorted into nouns, adjectives and verbs. Subsequently, nouns, adjectives and verbs are to be used to form sentences. In order, main sentences, subordinate clauses, command sentences, declarative sentences and interrogative sentences are formed by pupils in the class, written on the board by the teacher at the same time, copied by the whole class and read out together. Now the pupils are asked to write stories and poems. Using their examples, the rules of grammar are explained and the stories are corrected first by the learner and then by the teacher.

8.7.4.2 Maths

In maths lessons, everything is taught to be able to grasp the basic arithmetic operations plus, minus, times, divided in the positive number range up to 1 million. A separate collection of formulas for maths is created. This collection grows into a dictionary of mathematics by the end of the school career. Every arithmetical operation is defined mathematically and formulated in terms of content. Sentences are to be built from functions. For example, "plus two (+2)" can mean: 2 have been added to a group of humans. "times four (*4)" can mean: The group now consists of four times as many people.

8.7.4.3 Font and design

In the lessons for writing and design, everything is taught to train accurate work. Since handwriting is the first craft that children learn, this training shapes their entire professional life. In order to develop a uniform, legible handwriting, the pupils are asked to choose their own texts, which they copy in the most beautiful script. Design is practised by copying pictures or photos as accurately as possible. More details can be found in the 1995 Baden-Württemberg curriculum for primary school in the subject "Writing and Design".

8.7.4.4 Ethics

Ethics classes teach everything that convinces crowds to behave similarly. The content is tailored to the domestic context, so mainly domestic authors are used as sources. In the first class, proverbs such as "He who digs a pit for others, falls into it himself", jokes or stories that carry a moral embassy are presented, discussed and applied to cases that have happened to children, the class or at school. In the second grade, Protestant ethics with its work ethic and Christianity with its charity and helpfulness follow. Time clocks and church clocks are looked at and compared. Aid organisations such as the Red Cross or church institutions are introduced and visited. In the third grade, philosophical ethics are introduced. For example, Kant's "Categorical Imperative" is introduced to the class as a self-experiment, works on morality and criticism by Friedrich Nietzsche, and the theories on sociology and power by Max Weber. Textbook publishers work with teachers and learners to prepare the writings in a child-friendly way. In fourth grade, the world religions are introduced and houses of worship, services and believers from Judaism, Islam, Hinduism, Buddhism and Christianity are visited. In class, all religious festivals of all world religions of a year are celebrated.

8.7.4.5 Sex education

The subject of sex education is only taught in the fourth grade. Human reproduction is presented in its entire course. It starts with puberty, the change of the body and mind through the growth of nerve tracts, hair and glands as well as the increased production of sex hormones for women and men. First, the growth processes in the body and brain are presented, which are the same for boys and girls. In particular, the course of the brain's development from the beginning of puberty around the age of ten to the end at around the age of 27 is the focus of attention. Newly developed neural pathways must be used as much as possible so that they become stable enough not to be broken down. Children are asked to express all their experience wishes in the comprehensive school and to choose suitable electives wherever possible and to contact the teachers there. Children should be made aware of the coming time of uncertainty and boredom due to increased brain power and how they can use or damage the new potentials. The feeling of love and lust and when it can be expressed, how and through what. Role plays in class are used to practise dating and how to unobtrusively ask about mutual interest in dating and which types are undesirable or punishable and why.

Only in the second half of the year does sexual maturity follow with the body structure of the male and female and the changes before and after puberty. Care should be taken to use many pictures and videos of real humans to show the difference in sexual organs in different humans. First show pictures of hands, what to do with them and how to wash them. This is followed by the same pictures for sexual organs. If the children have a different reaction to the pictures, they are asked why this is so. So what makes the difference between hands and sexual organs. This is followed by a short excursion into the history of mankind's handling of sexual organs and clothing. How in prehistoric times everyone was naked, like animals today, how the sexual organs became a religious taboo, how it is today and what constitutes the free-body culture (nudism). This is followed by a discussion of how to use sexual organs, how to wash them thoroughly and what diseases can occur and when. The techniques of human reproduction are presented from getting to know each other, courtship behaviour, actions leading to sexual arousal, masturbation, sexual intercourse with orgasms in women and men, to fertilisation of the egg by sperm. In one hour, sex as a recreational pleasure is presented and why contraceptives and subcultures are necessary to recognise the existing natural sexual drive of humans without taboos within the framework of the constitution. The need for sex occurs more frequently in humans than would be necessary to keep population numbers the same. A birth rate of 2.1 children per woman replaces both parents and 0.1 children reflects mortality when humans die before reproducing. An understanding of both is to be awakened in the children. Staff from the Ministry of Family Affairs visit the class for a lesson to point out their assistance and directives in finding a partner. Pregnancy from implantation of the fertilised egg to birth is shown only in an animated film. The psyche of an infant and the early development of the brain and sensory organs are discussed in more detail. This is to give children a classification of their own psyche and brain power, what they have behind them and what still lies ahead. Children from the first to third class level may participate in these lessons if they have had or will have a sibling.

8.7.4.6 People's Computer

People's Computers is only taught in the fourth grade. The pupils receive their People's Computers here, but must leave them at school until their 10th birthday. This People's Computer becomes the state gift to every nationals on their 10th birthday, presented ceremoniously at school.

In this subject, pupils learn how to handle the device, the intranet and the directories. In particular, the Persons, Families and Education Directory is explained in detail, because these three directories are used for all data entries that have been made about the child by the state up to now. Most communication will take place in these directories, because this is where caregivers and peers can be online.

In class, as a project, the children are to re-enact an election of persons and a People's Committee in their own class and everyone has a say with their People's Computer.

8.7.4.7 Art[105]

In art lessons, new materials are introduced every lesson with which to create art. These are pencils made of wood, plastic and wax, brushes for water, oil and acrylic paint, as well as scissors, glue, hot glue, staplers, tape, paper, cardboard, saws, plastic, wood and metal. Works of art are never given a rating lower than 4. This is to show children the freedom of art and that everyone finds art beautiful in different ways. Failure in this subject is only possible if the student refuses to cooperate.

8.7.4.8 Sport[106]

In physical education, running, climbing and swimming are offered in a wide variety of games. They run in handball, football, basketball, dodgeball or ultimate frisbee. Climbing is done on trees, climbing walls and ropes. Swimming is done in the local swimming pool, lakes and rivers that are suitable for it. Sport should also be done during the short breaks between lessons, as long as there are no class room changes. The students learn the techniques of stretching, loosening and tensing in physical education lessons. They perform the exercises independently, with children from their class being elected as exercise leaders.

8.7.4.9 Music[107]

In music class, the first thing that is practised is humming and singing. The national anthem is the first song to be learned by heart. After that, the pupils are allowed to wish for songs in the national language to sing along to and vote on them. Once an awareness of rhythm and melody has been created, the introduction of musical instruments begins.

105§184.5 Promotion of music, sport, film, culture and art: BV Art.69
106§184.2 Promotion of music, sport, film, culture and art: BV Art.68
107§184.1 Promotion of music, sport, film, culture and art: BV Art.67a

Each school is expected to have melodic and rhythmic musical instruments, but of different types. There is a regular exchange of instruments. Music programmes are installed in the school's computer room. Each class should produce a song at least once a school year and send it to the Ministry of Media Affairs. On the intranet, the songs can be rated by all users and published in the primary school charts in the Media Directory and on the group page of the participating primary schools. The songs also run on the school radio. Once a year, the third classes organise an orchestra together with at least one other primary school.

8.7.4.10 Homeland and subject lessons

The homeland and subject lessons are a mixture of the basics from geography, history, natural history, politics and economics. The basics, however, remain limited to regional or national scope. It is only in the comprehensive school that one looks beyond this area.

Homeland and subject lessons have a question time once a week in which all questions relating to how and why certain things work may be asked. The teacher then has a week to investigate the questions via the Internet and Knowledge Directory or to obtain information via university enquiries. Questions that can be answered directly will be answered immediately.

8.7.4.11 Textile work

In the lessons for textile handicrafts, students learn and practise how to make all household items themselves. Sewing by hand and with the sewing machine, spinning, weaving, knitting and crocheting are learned on different textiles, but at least with hemp, sheep's wool and cotton. The techniques are practised by making your own clothes and cuddly toys.

8.7.4.12 Craft

In the craft lessons, students learn how to make furniture out of wood, how to make crockery out of clay, how to lay electricity including switches and how to generate electricity with a dynamo. If possible, this subject should last 4 school hours at a stretch in order to reduce the long preparation times and already simulate half a working day. The times of the big break remain the same.

8.7.5 Project week

Before the summer holidays, there is a project week at every primary school. The topics of the projects are proposed by the pupils and selected by the teachers. For this purpose, topics or product suggestions are made and listed by all pupils. This list is then voted on. Votes from teachers are displayed separately, because these votes symbolise that a teacher has knowledge in this subject or is willing to do investigation for preparation. In the previous week, these election processes are completed and the students vote themselves into their project groups. These projects take place for one week during school time. The projects may be extended for a maximum of one week if teachers are necessary. If parents can prove to teachers that they can and want to continue to lead the project, the parents take over the supervision and guidance of the project group. If enough parents can be found, the project can be run for the entire holiday period. The children in afternoon care can vote on whether their current projects from afternoon care should continue.

8.7.6 Project day

One afternoon a week is used to offer projects that run throughout the school year. Participation is not compulsory, but can be ordered by the teacher in case of poor performance. The projects must always use skills from at least one school subject. The topics of the projects are decided by the primary school pupils themselves. To this end, each pupil requests a topic, all pupils rate all topics and in the final vote it is decided whether individual groups do different projects or whether the whole school or even several educational institutions, do a joint project.

8.8 Afternoon care

All pupils who stay at school in the afternoon because their parents work or because the children want to of their own accord go to afternoon care.

The care concept is either based on that of a nursery school or an all-day class. If a team of 2 educators gets along well and wants to work together for 4 years, they take over a full-day class from enrolment to grade 4. In a full-day class, all the children in a class are looked after by the class teacher and the team of 2 educators throughout the day. Only during school holidays is the class broken up and the children of all ages are cared for in the open concept of a nursery school.

Whether a child is cared for in the afternoon according to the concept of an all-day class or a nursery school is decided by the child, parents, teachers and educators. Parents ask their children before they start school and report them. Children are allowed to decide once during their primary school years whether they want to be cared for in the all-day class or as in a nursery school. Teachers and educators decide whether a child needs a regular or less regular daily structure to learn better. They then propose a change to one or the other concept to the child and the parents.

Childcare is provided at the primary school. If there are not at least 20 children and 2 caregivers for afternoon care, the few primary school children are cared for after school at the nearest local nursery school. After school hours, classrooms are used for homework, playing, exercising, painting, craft and making music. Equipment for the afternoon is stored in a warehouse, but can also be used in the mornings, for example during breaks. The children can choose to join groups, leisure activities and projects. If the number of participants is limited or a group size has to remain the same for a long time, unwilling participants can swap with volunteers or friends. Teachers, educators and voluntary retirees are used for supervision. The afternoon is structured so that parents can pick up their children at any time or set a time when their children can go home alone. A change of these times is only possible 3 times a year.

8.8.1 Lunch

Lunch takes place after the school hours of the morning. Depending on the size and equipment of the school, the food is delivered or prepared on site. The children eat with reusable cutlery. Whenever possible, the children are assigned to kitchen duties. Table manners are to be practised during meals so that they can eat in any restaurant in the world.

After lunch, there is a movement break. Here the children should be able to play freely and lend out toys if needed. In turns, children are assigned to rearrange the classrooms during the movement break in order to prepare them for afternoon care.

8.8.2 Homework

Each primary school pupil is required to do 60 minutes of homework and learning per school day. Still work and partner work take place in different rooms. Homework in partner work is specially made for afternoon care children. When the afternoon care children do their homework is up to them as long as they have chosen the open concept. Otherwise, the time is predetermined. Children who are taken to the special primary school have to do homework and study for an hour before bedtime if necessary.

8.8.2.1 Homework mentors

Those who have finished their homework put a sign saying "Done" on their seat and work on their study folder until another student comes up to them and asks for help. To do this, you have to take your homework, stand up, walk over, tap on your shoulder and walk out the door together. Questions are then clarified in front of the door. The teacher makes sure that after the "help" everything has not already been said and the pupil is finished immediately.

8.8.3 Leisure

During free time, games are offered in which the pupils learn to abide by the rules of the game, to play as a team and also to learn to lose. During this time, the educators, teachers and pensioners exercise the duty of supervision on behalf of the parents. They are guided by the child's well-being and the respective developmental stage of the child. The educators take over the professional observation and documentation in order to evaluate the developmental stages of the individual children. In cooperation with the college where the educator has been trained, all observations, documentations and subsequent leisure activities or projects for the children are evaluated as social science data. All recognised abilities, knowledge, weaknesses and strengths of a child are listed and categorised. The categories are linked to a child's physical and mental development, for example, gross and fine movements, thinking, questioning and deciding on the basis of categories, rules, laws, reasons for evidence and counter-arguments. From all the entries, the colleges create a collection of games with leisure activities and projects that can promote different strengths or mitigate weaknesses.

8.8.3.1 Game collection

The game collection is available in the Knowledge Directory and can also be used by adults to strengthen similar physical or mental strengths or to weaken weaknesses that occur throughout life. All users are asked to indicate if an offer or project was helpful to them in order to conduct the study with even more age groups. All users can categorise themselves and be supported by an algorithm. Those who fill out the educators' observation forms for themselves can automatically be shown which measures might help or interest them. If more than one person is needed, a group can be used to automatically search for members who have indicated similar strengths or weaknesses and also search for persons for corresponding measures via the Knowledge Directory. An anonymous search can be started via a function. The algorithm searches for all persons within a certain radius who have similar strengths or weaknesses and sends them a request to join a support group. The person who initiates the request can choose whether or not to include their data from the Persons Directory and their profile picture. Likewise, the group members can reply anonymously and write in the group, so that the name and profile picture are not shown to the users.

The play collection is a group in the Knowledge Directory. Each offer or project has a profile. The description must state how something is done and what is promoted. This makes it easier for users to indicate where they have strengths or weaknesses and receive suitable proposals for promotion. The description is automatically keyworded by an algorithm. The keywords are displayed to the creator of the profile. He can remove those that do not apply and add those that do. As an example of professional execution, the following is the profile: "Producing a film" for humans from the age of 4 with the minimum number of 2 persons.

8.8.3.1.1 Project example: Producing a film[108]

In this project, children produce a feature film together and with the support of their caregivers in the primary school. It should be noted that according to the situational approach and the project idea, the children have the possibility to change or end the project at any time through a committee. All that is needed is an initiative by a majority of children. For educators who have doubts, there is the possibility of a vote of confidence at every meeting and a vote on the continuation of the project.

The same procedure can be used to create a photo story or a radio play. For a photo story, steps 7 (filming) to 8 (editing) are

---

108§184.3 Promotion of music, sport, film, culture and art: BV Art.71

omitted and replaced by a step in which photos or paintings and speech bubbles are made and inserted into a notebook. Step 6 (training) is omitted, except for c) (making stage and costumes).

For a radio play, step 6 (training) is adapted. Section b) (camera technology) is reduced to sound technology, c) (making stage and costumes) is omitted. Step 7 (filming) is replaced by sound recording.

1.   Topic identification: (plenary)

The plenary names popular topics. Educators list them and put them to the plenary for election. Each child has two votes and one vote may not be given to their own topic. In this way, autonomy is promoted through self-determination of the topic proposals and solidarity is achieved by giving votes to other people's proposals. The understanding of democracy is trained by dividing the votes.

2.   History invention: (group work)

Adventures that characters could experience together are invented by the children, spoken out, acted out and one educator each records the expressions of the children in the group he or she is in charge of. By inventing adventures, perspective-taking is strengthened. The children put themselves in the shoes of the character. Together with their self-selected group, their joy of communication is promoted. Competence is generated by revealing, discussing and realising or discarding proposals in a group. Competent handling of the situation can inspire the inventiveness of the group.

3.   Script development: (plenary)

The recorded stories of all groups are read out one after the other and the group members are allowed to add additions. At the end of the session, the plenary votes on the most popular story. For minority protection, parts of the second and third placed stories can also be included, for example in the form of characters, settings or individual actions. Language competence increases through listening to and comparing the content of the different stories. Creativity, imagination and linguistic expression are especially needed when linking stories. The protection of minorities is the basis of every democracy and should help to reconcile exuberant winners and saddened losers.

4.   Storyboard development: (group work)

At the beginning there is input on image setting from the wide range to the detail shot and the division of an image in the golden section. The screenplay is divided into parts of approximately equal length and each group takes over one part. The script text is transformed into environments, roles and speech texts. Children choose locations, take photos, pictures or sketches of them and play the speaking parts in an improvised play. Educators write down the speech text in the storyboard. In the storyboard, the picture or photo, location, setting, speech text, emotion and costume of the actors are listed next to each other in columns. All groups put their individual parts together to form the whole storyboard. This phase of work is characterised by artistic design and aesthetics as well as the effect of language, emphasis, facial expressions and gestures in communication. The composition of a scene or a shot is a representation of the imagination and takes on its own aesthetic through the alternation of close and distant perspectives as well as changing sets and costumes.

5.   Castings: (plenary)

Voluntary children can choose any role in front of the camera. Multiple choices are possible. Each child learns his or her role and plays it for the rest of the group. It starts with the main roles and ends with the supporting roles. Once all the candidates have auditioned for a role, they have to leave the room and the rest vote on who played the role best. This voting can also take place in the presence of the candidates, but as a secret election on slips of paper. All candidates are assigned a colour, which is drawn on a white sheet, which is folded and put into an opaque ballot box.

The tasks behind the camera are not assigned in castings. The children pin their passport photos next to the pictograms of the tasks. A change is possible at any time and only needs to be voted with the other child.

The castings demand autonomy, solidarity and competence in equal measure. The children themselves decide which roles or tasks they apply for. In doing so, they are dependent on their community. What ultimately convinces their community, however, is their competence to make their role credible to the plenary through language, tone of voice and gestures. However, the auditions are also a litmus test and cause disappointment, so care must be taken to ensure confidentiality, especially in the voting process. Especially socially competent children like to give comfort here and thus experience confirmation and gratitude for their willingness to help.

6.   Training: (group work)

During the training, all children are asked in plenary if their parents could help and if certain material should be collected and brought along over a longer period of time.

a) Acting lessons: An educator reads a book aloud. The actors first listen and then, after about one page, act out the characters mentioned. The children choose the books themselves.

Language and literacy are particularly promoted here. The children's role-playing phase is productively taken up here and their empathy skills are further developed.

b) Camera equipment: An educator orders all the camera, lighting, sound, electricity, tripods and a computer including an editing programme from the Ministry of Media Affairs. Together with the equipment, a training team comes to show the participants involved how to handle the equipment and picks them up again at an agreed time. The handling of camera, light and sound is practised. As an exercise, a short documentary film is made with a smartphone.

Media and communication technology shape these workshops and turn children and educators into learning, researching and discovering work partners.

c) Making the stage and costumes: An educator advises on the election of the means of production and assists with the procurement and processing of the means. The children find out what the characters look like or think up the stage set. They create costumes from carnival costumes and old clothes and the stage set from furniture, handicraft material, packaging material or bulky waste.

Here, the visual and performing arts are promoted as well as environmental awareness and life practice. Particular attention is paid to solidarity, as collection actions by a group can help individual crafters achieve better results.

d) Film music: With the music teacher, the film music is composed and sounds are dubbed. An aesthetic overall composition of moving pictures and spoken texts includes the accentuated background music and sounds. The musical transport of moods and cultures is made tangible for the children.

7. Film shooting (plenary and group)

The educators support the directors, camera operators and filming supervisors in their tasks. The children can divide into groups and shoot scenes at different locations. Children without a current task can watch or otherwise enjoy themselves. During filming, the creative use of the premises comes into its own. The group room becomes a stage, the office a back-stage area, the toilet a changing room, the dining room a lounge with snacks, the sports hall a stunt arena and the forest an open-air stage. For a short time, the children experience the everyday working life of the humans whose products they consume almost daily.

8. Editing (group or individual work)

The educators provide the editing computer, make sure it is used correctly and let voluntary children edit the film with it. The educators do the rest of the interfacing themselves.

Mathematics, logic, technology and aesthetics come together in this task. Children and educators are usually equally learners here. Having the patience to familiarise oneself with a technical programme and to assemble the film from individual parts promotes frustration tolerance as well as logical understanding. Since each shot should be seen for about four to five seconds, small arithmetical tasks arise on the timeline of the editing programme.

9.   Reflection and revision (plenary)

The edited film is shown to the whole group and they are asked what was learned, when, how and why. They are asked what they liked and didn't like, why and what should be done differently next time. The educators let the children tell what they enjoyed most and least about the project and what they think they know now that they did not know before.

Final requests for changes to the film can be made, discussed and voted on. Through reflection, the children can take a step onto the meta-level to visualise their learning process and draw conclusions for their personal future.

10.   Documentation and presentation (plenary)

For the presentation, credits are made by filming each child in their costume or with their work equipment and introducing themselves and their task in the film. The educators have documented the phases with photos in the course of the project and create a slide show for the credits. The children's families are invited to the institution to watch the film, the credits and the making-of slide show together. Each child receives a copy of the file on their profile in the Education Directory.

The family is involved in the child's experience, usually the children have been talking about the project at home for a long time and the parents are interested to see the result.

8.8.4 Clubs

The primary school cooperates with surrounding clubs that accept children of primary school age. Clubs are allowed to use the primary school's premises if enough children want to take part in their activities. If children need to travel to the club's premises, car pools can be formed or a school bus can be used. The care provided by a club is settled via the child benefit.

8.8.5 Voluntary pensioners

Local senior citizens and retirement homes are invited to come to the primary school on afternoons of their election to read to the students, tell them things, answer questions or play table games.

8.8.6 Pickup

Children who have not yet been picked up by their parents by closing time, or who cannot go home overnight, are picked up by the transport service of the nearest special primary school. There, the children receive dinner and help with the preparation and washing up. Before going to bed, the children can listen to music or audio books via headphones or read.

9 Comprehensive school

The comprehensive school is a mixture of primary school and college. It is divided into learning years 5 to 10 and final years 11 to 13. 18 subjects are offered during the 6 learning years, in which a maximum of 6 certificates can be obtained per subject. The subjects are national language, maths, sports, economics, music, computer science, chemistry, physics, biology, geography, technology, crafts, politics, history, psychology, ethics, foreign languages and art. Foreign languages offered are English, German, Spanish, French, Russian and Chinese, whereby each educational institution must offer at least 3 foreign languages.

In school years 5 to 11, 7 one-year subjects must be taken, which are linked to the respective learning year. The one-year subjects are learning, inventing, choosing, integration, nutrition, applying for a job and building a house.

Subjects are taught in courses by teachers, selected by learners in their timetable and rewarded with a certificate. To earn a certificate, the corresponding central performance record must be passed with a grade of 4 or better.

9.1 Hours per week

The fifth learning year is an introductory year in which all 18 subjects and one year-long subject must be taken, but each subject is taught for only one hour per week. This corresponds to 19 hours per week. How many subjects learners take per semester after the introductory year is up to them. A minimum of 20 lessons per week is prescribed.

The Examinations Office provides lists of required subjects and certificates for each final examination. The subjects required for a particular degree are determined by the curriculum and the requirements of the Examinations Office. If an educational institution wishes to have an educational focus, it can specify compulsory and optional subjects and how many certificates must be obtained per subject.

9.2 Certificates

The certificates provide evidence of the acquisition of skills. The skills are tested in the central performance records and a certificate is awarded if the student passes. However, the content of the courses is not bound to the certificates, but can go beyond them. For example, those who can acquire all the mathematical skills in physics and economics do not have to attend the courses in maths, but can participate directly in the central performance record for maths, where the corresponding skills are tested.

The aim should be for teachers to work across subjects as much as possible and to teach the contents of several subjects at the same time in one course. In this way, learning content can be learned in a shorter time. Teachers and learners are free to decide how content from different subjects is combined and thus how long it takes to acquire a certificate. The only thing that matters is that the content is sufficient to pass the central performance record. All teachers are to coordinate their content in the teachers' council and teach overlaps together. Educational institutions are thus competing to teach as many skills as possible in as short a time as possible. Whether learners then leave the educational institution earlier or attend additional courses and acquire certificates in them is up to them.

Learners can collect different certificates depending on which qualification they are aiming for. With the minimum of 20 hours per week, only the basic qualification can be achieved. If the learner's educational aspirations change during the course of the comprehensive schooling, the necessary certificates can be made up. Since certificates are not linked to a learning year, except for those in the one-year subjects. This makes it possible to make a decision for a different qualification at any time through a learning year with many hours per week.

Prior knowledge may be necessary for the acquisition of certain certificates, which must first be acquired through other certificates. When describing a course, prerequisite certificates must be indicated. When creating the timetable, it is automatically recognised if a student does not yet have the necessary prior knowledge to acquire a certificate. Registration is then not possible.

9.3 Teaching method

In each subject, a choice can be made between the teaching method of frontal teaching, project teaching or free learning. Teachers adapt their teaching methods to the wishes and learning types of the learners. Teachers must be proficient in all three teaching methods, but can indicate their subject specialisations and preferences for certain teaching methods in their profile in the Education Directory. Educational institutions can offer focal points for certain teaching methods if motivated teachers are enthusiastic about the same teaching method.

9.3.1 Projects

Projects can be carried out independently by learners as part of the teaching method of project teaching, free learning or outside of class time. Projects in project teaching and free learning always have certain requirements to meet the curriculum. Learners can offer voluntary projects and form project groups, but are not bound by the curriculum.

For all projects that can be carried out for companies, entrepreneurs enter their wishes in the project collection. Learners can also choose projects from these and earn money with them if they are successful. The parts for a production on behalf of a company are obtained through the company. The companies give concrete information about the final product, but not about the production. The learners should first create a production line themselves. When they have finished, they send it to the company, which checks whether their own production line is more efficient or whether work steps are taken over. If the learners' production line is not more efficient, the company's deposited production line is used. The prior deposit already happens when the company enters its project into the project collection. In case the learners' production line is more efficient, it will be tested by the learners. If the production is indeed more efficient, learners have invented an innovation. If industrial property rights arise from the innovations, the responsible learners must be included in the list of inventors and can become licensors. Thus, an ongoing income can be generated through licence sales already during the school career.

For all projects that are to take place within the framework of the classroom, but additional expert knowledge is required due to the choice of topic, guest lecturers from companies and colleges can be engaged for individual lessons. For voluntary projects carried out exclusively by minors, an adult supervisor must be organised who is either an honorary service or a parent of a minor learner.

9.3.1.1 Mobile Innovation Labs

In order to be able to carry out a project appropriately, a laboratory may be necessary. Projects addressing future challenges can order one of the appropriate mobile Innovation Labs from the Ministry of Innovation[109] . The equipment of each mobile Innovation Lab can be found on the intranet

109 Ministry of Innovation - 6.5 Mobile Innovation Labs

site of the Ministry of Innovation. If possible, several courses should benefit from the Innovation Lab and hold part of their classes there. The Innovation Lab provides the necessary consumables when ordered and paid for by the participants. Project participants can also bring parts themselves at any time. Depending on the project, parts can be supplied and paid for directly by companies if it is a project from the project collection. If it is a project from the Research Cost Fund, the components are also provided free of charge because companies have paid money into this fund to have things researched.

9.3.1.2 Research groups

Independent research groups can be formed from the project groups, which freely choose their members, because anyone can leave the group if they wish and new members can be accepted. The members of these voluntary research groups can be pupils of this school or any other citizen. Underage members need the consent of their parents, which can be saved on the child's ID card in the intranet café.

An interface with the People's Innovation Company Think Tank[110] is created because this research lab is outsourced from the school administration after opening hours and is taken over by the People's Innovation Company Think Tank. This gives each project the opportunity to continue or even be marketed worldwide.

9.4 Type of teaching

Certificates can be offered by teachers in one block or in weekly courses held for six months or a whole year. The learners occupy these events in their timetable and thus signal their demand for the corresponding type of teaching. If there are conflicts, a committee must find a regularisation and put it to a vote.

In weekly classes, courses for subjects repeat weekly on the

110Ministry of Innovation - 11 People's Innovation Company Think Tank same date for a half-year or with half the number of lessons per week for a year.

In block teaching, one and the same subject is taught over days or weeks in order to acquire a certificate in the shortest possible time. Block teaching is offered at all comprehensive schools during the holidays. At educational institutions with a focus on block teaching, the entire school year can be taught in blocks. For example, all the content of mathematics lessons could be taught in one year if all 6 certificates for mathematics were taught in 6 consecutive teaching blocks. In the timetable of this year, hardly any other courses would then be possible. If it is the wish of a large number of learners at an educational institution, entire school subjects can be offered in one block. The educational institutions decide independently in committees and voting how the teaching content is to be packaged in terms of time.

No matter which type of teaching is chosen, the dates for the central performance record are the same everywhere and are issued by the Examinations Office. This means that there may be a gap of 11 months between the block teaching and the central performance record. If, however, it turns out that block teaching and weekly teaching are in roughly equal demand, the Examinations Office must develop 2 central performance records per year or offer the dates per learning year in a subject in transfer.

9.5 Breaks

The only requirement for the timing of lessons is that there should be sufficient breaks. On average, there should be a 15-minute break every 45 minutes. In voting with the learners, teachers can adapt the break times to their needs. If breaks are not taken, the lesson will end earlier. If the learners unanimously agree, the break times can be omitted or postponed as desired. This should make it possible to distribute the lesson content according to the current receptivity of the learners.

9.6 Change of school

Students are allowed to change comprehensive schools up to three times on their own initiative, for example to gain certificates in a certain type of teaching. If they have problems with teachers or classmates or have a partner at the other school, they can change schools once additionally. To do this, a student must first look for a new school and apply to the new headmaster. This can be done via the Education Directory, because every headmaster has a profile there that every pupil can write to. By clicking on the "Application" button, the applicant makes his or her school file available to the new headmaster. If they are suitable, they are invited to an interview. If the interview is successful, the new headmaster calls the old headmaster and, if there are no objections, the change of school is completed. Now the pupil can enter his or her change of school in the Education Directory Profile and the new headmaster confirms it. If there are objections and the application is rejected, the student can lodge an appeal with the Education Authority. A change of school can also be ordered by the punitive measure "expulsion from school".

9.7 Computers for the lessons

From comprehensive school onwards, students are expected to use their People's Computer as a computer in class. There are stations in schools where People's Computers can be connected to use the keyboard, mouse and screen and join a school network. While binding to the school's own devices, the People's Computer's functions are blocked and only the programmes for teaching are accessible. The People's Computer accesses the intranet and calls up programmes running on the Ministry of Education's servers via the intranet connection. These include programmes for electronic data processing, image editing, music composition or film editing. These programmes either come from the open source community or are programmed by the Ministry of Digital Affairs. The writing programme automatically detects spelling mistakes and marks them with a red wavy line under the word. This auto-correction is switched off for performance records. Anyone who breaks their People's Computer or additional material is immediately given replacement equipment, which they must pay for or work off if necessary.

9.8 Seating arrangement

Usually there is no seating arrangement. There must always be enough tables and chairs for all learners who have registered for the course through their timetable. If necessary, there is a store of folding chairs including folding tables. In each course, the tables and chairs can be placed as they are needed. If a majority of a course is in favour of a seating arrangement, it will be specified by a course committee.

9.9 Transfer

It is possible to have to repeat certificates. If the grade in a subject is above 4, the corresponding course in that subject must be repeated. All required subjects must be completed before the final examination. In order to be able to catch up on subjects, courses in all subjects may be attended at any time. This makes it possible, for example, if you do badly in maths and well in the national language in one semester, to attend the courses from two year groups in the national language at the same time. This gives the student more time in the following semester to attend mathematics classes in different forms, provided the teachers' duty rosters permit this.

It is possible to skip subjects. If the grade in a subject is 1.0, one can take part in the central performance record of the coming year already in the current year and must attend the date for the written re-examination for the current year. If both examinations are passed with 1.0, a learning year in the subject can be skipped. The pupil then attends the next higher year group for the teaching of this subject. Those who attend the comprehensive school up to the college entrance qualification then have the opportunity to start a distance learning course in this subject at the end, which the teacher of this subject helps with. However, the final examination in this subject does not change for these students. Those who have skipped all subjects once can bring forward the final examination and leave the comprehensive school earlier.

9.10 Timetable

In the 5th learning year, the timetable is set by the educational institution because all subjects are taught. In the first lesson of the first week, there is a survey in each subject to find out who prefers which teaching method. All students with the same teaching method get together with the appropriate teacher in a course and from then on attend the courses together.

From the 6th learning year onwards, students must create their own timetable in the Education Directory and, after an introductory week, register bindingly for their subjects in the coming semester.

In the first week of a new school year, there are all the subjects offered at the educational institution. The teachers and the subjects may not duplicate each other, so if there are four maths teachers, these teachers may not hold their first introductory lesson at the same time in the first week. The students should choose their teachers. If a teacher is shunned by students of all year groups for more than 2 half years, he/she will be transferred to another educational institution. If this happens again, termination will follow.

In the introductory lessons, the content of this course is presented, the upcoming performance records and how they can be completed to earn the certificate. The students then decide for themselves whether they want to study an elective subject or an in-depth study of a compulsory subject and with which teacher.

The times and rooms for the offers are provisionally fixed. If there is overcrowding, the course will be offered twice or shuttled to another school. If a course is under-subscribed, it will not take place or will be shuttled. If a course is oversubscribed and neither more space nor more teachers can be offered, nor can it be shuttled to another educational institution, the less well-attended courses must be attended.

Those who cannot take the desired certificate with the desired teacher due to overcrowding have the opportunity to participate in a request and bonus system via the Education Directory. This system prevents the same students from not being able to attend desired courses more than once.

9.11 Tutoring

Learners who have already completed a certificate will tutor those learners who are in the process of completing that certificate. Those with good grades in a certificate will be placed at the top of the tutoring list. The tutoring list is listed in the Education Directory in the group of the respective course. Learners can choose other learners to tutor them here. Potential tutors can also decline a request. Students who are asked to tutor but do not do so will receive a lower grade in the next certificate for that subject. Those who give private tuition will receive a quarter of a grade better in the next certificate in that subject. Tutoring is voluntary, but may be ordered by a teacher in the event of poor grades on the second attempt to obtain a particular certificate. Tutoring takes place during opening hours at the educational institution, but can also take place at a learner's home. A tutor may provide tutoring to one or more tutoring students. These sessions are called tutorials and the tutors are called tutors. If there are 10 or more tutoring students, the Social Market Economy minimum wage is paid. If a student passes the certificate with a grade of at least 2, the tutor receives half a grade better in the next certificate in that subject. Those who have given private tuition will have this noted in their testimonial. Tutoring is basically an honourary service and an act of solidarity among learners, especially for those with very good grades.

9.12 Canteen

Students can have breakfast in the canteen between 7am and 8am, lunch between 10am and 4pm and dinner between 6pm and 8pm. Meals are served on trays with washable dishes and can be eaten at tables in the assembly hall or elsewhere on the school premises. Trays and dishes must be returned to the canteen afterwards. Issue and return are confirmed by the identity card. Payment is automatically settled at the cash desk via the identity card and the child benefit. If it is take-away food, the return is not required. It is possible to use dishes that you have brought yourself. Learners at educational centres in Social Villages visit the commercial kitchen.[111]

The food that is processed and served in the canteen comes either from the school garden, from taxes paid in kind or from supermarkets that have to deliver their goods that have reached the expiry date to the canteen without interrupting the cold chain. If this food is not sufficient, one-year supply contracts are concluded with local farmers and food businesses of the Social Market Economy.

9.13 Opening hours

The comprehensive schools open at 8 am and close at 8 pm. After 8pm, occupancy can be by clubs, citizens or the People's Innovation Company Think Tank. During these 12 hours, teachers and learners teach and learn in jointly coordinated duty rosters and timetables. Minors have the option of being taken to the nearest Social Village after closing by a transport service or by public transport if parents are not at home. In the morning, these minors are brought back to school. Regular overnight stays at the children's home of the nearest Social Village are not possible. In this case, the comprehensive school in the Social Village must be attended.

9.14 Free time in the all-day school

During free periods, or if classes end early, learners can attend all other courses at the comprehensive school. Fruit and water are available in the canteen throughout the day. In the assembly hall there is a cupboard with board games that can be played at the tables or outside, as well as table football.

---

111 Ministry of Planned Economy - 9.4.3 Commercial kitchen

Once a year there is a school festival where all the courses present their projects, sell drinks and food and play dance music. After passing their final exams, graduates can have a graduation party or prom at the educational institution.

9.15 School subjects

The school subjects are divided into one-year and multi-year subjects. For some, only one certificate can be obtained, for others up to six certificates. One-year subjects are learning, inventing, voting, integration, nutrition, applying for a job and building a house. Multi-year subjects are national language, maths, physical education, economics, music, computer science, chemistry, physics, biology, geography, technology, crafts, politics, history, psychology, ethics, foreign languages and art. The foreign languages are English, German, Spanish, French, Russian and Chinese.

9.15.1 One-year subjects

One-year school subjects are subjects that are only taught for one year. They are timed according to the need for pupils and their age.

9.15.1.1 Subject in the fifth learning year: Learning

In the subject Learning, different learning methods are tried out and tested in short tests. The different methods and types of teaching at the comprehensive school are presented, tried out and linked to the different types of learning.

Learning and working through tasks are broken down into work steps. The first step is to take in knowledge and create a useful summary of it. In the second step, parts from the summaries are put together to develop a mock exam including a sample solution. In the third step, the mock exam is repeated several times and corrected using the sample solution until no more faults occur.

People have different strengths and each human learns

fastest with his or her strengths. One also speaks of talent. It is important to identify talents in youths at an early stage in order to give them a goal at their pubescent age that can hardly disappoint them. That is why surveys are conducted in the classroom. What kind of thinking or acting is easy for the respondents is the focus of interest. For example, mathematical theorems with formulae and equations, pictorial imagination, sense of navigation and orientation, social connections, language, talking, sports, working on a PC or crafts. As a result for the survey, the pupils are shown which method they can learn most easily with and which subjects or educational qualifications they might be particularly interested in.

9.15.1.2 School subject in the sixth learning year: Inventing

In the invention lessons, the entire invention process is carried out, from the invention in a Think Tank[112] to the application for a suitable industrial property right to the founding of a company and marketing as a project. Permanent homework is to keep an idea diary for a year. In each lesson, new ideas are read out if pupils have had an idea since the last lesson. Students learn to sort ideas into categories such as business ideas, technical or social inventions, game ideas, fantastic ideas and others. Different types of ideas are sorted according to their innovativeness.

All participants agree to maintain confidentiality and sign a non-disclosure agreement. The patent camera is used in every lesson to be able to clarify afterwards who had which idea and how big the share of further developments of participants is.

Class visits are conducted by professionals responsible for inventions, such as Innovation Agency staff, patent attorneys, patent examiners, research engineers or chemists from companies.

Classes include visits to a People's Innovation Company Think Tank, mobile Innovation Labs[113] and Innovation Workshops

---

112 Ministry of Innovation - 11 People's Innovation Company Think Tank

113 Ministry of Innovation - 6.5 Mobile Innovation Labs

in Social Villages[114] .

9.15.1.2.1 Innovation project

Each student writes his idea face down on a piece of paper and pockets it. Then he goes to the blackboard and writes it on the back so that the students don't see it. This creates a list of ideas that no one knows who came up with them. The class votes on the most popular idea. Everyone has 2 votes and is not allowed to give 2 votes to any idea. The idea with the most votes is discussed and how it could best be implemented. The inventor of the idea is announced at the end by reporting and showing their piece of paper. The class works out a provisional patent together, reports it to the town hall and goes through the whole protection process. This project first takes place in the sixth learning year and is taken up in project teaching in the tenth and thirteenth learning years in the appropriate subject so that volunteers from the project can start a company with the idea or sell the invention under licence.

9.15.1.3 School subject in the seventh learning year: Integration

Students learn what constitutes a culture, subculture, language, nationality, race, ethnicity and human kind. Role plays are used to learn the meanings of hospitality, immigration, emigration, foreigner and inland, integration and assimilation and how they can be interpreted differently. Communication techniques, such as Watzlawick's 5 axioms[115] or the 4 sides of a news according to Schulz von Thun[116] , are also practised in role plays. Part of the lesson is also an introduction to the laws of the Ministry of Integration, its measures and the voting on the quota of foreigners. In the class excursion, an integration measure and the Integration Office in the town hall are

114 Ministry of Planned Economy - 10.9.4 Innovation workshops and laboratories
115 https://www.paulwatzlawick.de/axiome.html
116 https://www.schulz-von-thun.de/die-modelle/das-kommunikationsquadrat

visited. As a project, a city rally for newcomers to the city will be planned and a test run will be carried out by the pupils.[117] A two-week student exchange is designed to provide an insight into different ways of life in the country. The student exchange takes place between schools in different parts of the city, so that children from poorer and richer neighbourhoods, with parents with or without a university degree, get to know the life of the other social class. Pupils can decide for themselves whether they want to do the exchange within the same city or within a radius of 10 to 20 kilometres. They can also decide whether they want to do the exchange with the same or the opposite sex. All exchange partners are in their seventh learning year. Keeping in touch and becoming friends may be possible. During this time, one student lives with the other student and attends their educational institution with them, but follows its own timetable at the other educational institution, only with different teachers and different classmates. After one week, the student moves to the other exchange partner's place of residence and after two weeks, the exchange is over.

9.15.1.4 School subject in the eighth learning year: Election

The school subject Elections teaches the political structure of the state and its political processes in which the citizens are involved. In role-plays, pupils take on the roles of party wing leaders, ministers, deputy ministers and candidates in the election campaign, including the development of an election programme. The students choose the topic themselves and thus decide which of the 18 ministries they would like to get to know better. They conduct quorums, committees and voting to practise the procedures of a direct democracy. Their People's Computer serves as a tool. At least one trip to the intranet café, including a tour of the voting computer, is part of the lesson.[118]

---

117 Ministry of Integration - 7.7 Integration measures, 5.2.1 Integration Office, 7 Immigration, 7.6.2.1 Guided tour of the city
118 Ministry of State Organisation - 8 Political structure, 9 Political processes

9.15.1.5 School subject in the ninth learning year: Nutrition

The school subject nutrition is about nutritional competence, which enables a healthy diet oriented towards the phases of life. Preventive measures in the area of nutrition are taught, with which one can adapt one's diet to the current phase of life. Students in this subject are always assigned to community catering services at the school. There, in addition to cooking and washing up, they also help to complete the nutrition research studies. The lessons on the food cycle start with sowing and harvesting, milling and baking, breeding and slaughtering and end with a cooking class. During the holidays at harvest time, students of this year group are employed as harvest helpers on farms of Social Market Economy[119] and receive the usual remuneration for harvest helpers, but have to pay 10% of it to the Ministry of Education.

9.15.1.6 School subject in the tenth learning year: Job application training

In the school subject Job Application, students learn how to write a cover letter and a CV, how to understand and write job references and how to register in the Labour Directory. Job interviews are role-played, including which questions are inadmissible. Once a year, companies are invited to the comprehensive school for a job fair. Here, all voluntary companies have a stand where they can advertise for interns and graduates. At least one internship of 2 weeks must be completed during the holidays. Excursions are made by bus. The bus takes students to volunteer companies for an hour and pilots about 7 companies a day.

---

119 Ministry of Social Market Economy - 14.4 Harvesters

9.15.1.7 School subject in the eleventh learning year: House building[120]

The school subject House Construction is about how to build, extend and repair houses during the eleventh learning year. The initial training contents and safety instructions of all craftspersons necessary for building a house are taught. During the holidays, 2 two-week work placements must be completed at one craft company each for exterior construction and interior finishing.

After the eleventh learning year, houses are built together with the Construction Team[121] for one year. The construction work starts at the beginning of the summer holidays. By winter, the exterior work is finished and the interior work lasts until spring. After that, the students have holidays until the twelfth learning year begins after the summer holidays. Graduates of the basic qualification leave the comprehensive school after the eleventh year of learning, are released from compulsory schooling after the construction of the house and start the People's Service.

9.15.2 Perennial subjects

A maximum of 6 certificates can be obtained for all multi-year subjects, which build on each other in some subjects.

All subjects that pupils can choose for themselves can be visited for a week the year before the election. In this way, they can look at all the interesting subjects the previous year and decide on a few. It is forbidden to influence children in their choice of subjects. Advice is permissible, but sentences for non-observance are not. Children can turn to the Youth Welfare Office in case of violations by guardians or teachers.

9.15.2.1 Maths

1.   The arithmetic operations plus, minus, times, divided are performed with negative numbers and brackets.

---

120 §226.1 Housing and home ownership promotion: BV Art. 108
121 Ministry of Infrastructure - 5.8 Construction Team

2. The arithmetic operations plus, minus, times, divided are performed with decimal places and fractions.

3. The arithmetic operations plus, minus, times, divided are performed with powers and roots.

4. All arithmetic operations and learned ways of performing them from the previous certificates are used to set up functions that are expressed in tables and coordinate systems.

5. All the mathematical possibilities learned are used to do probability theory and game theory.

6. All the mathematical possibilities learned are used to simulate processes of any kind with the help of the curve discussion.

9.15.2.2 National language

1. Taking notes during a narration is practised with the help of dictation, as is standardised note-taking in the form of a protocol or report.

2. Oral and written retelling of classic domestic literature is practised, as well as ancient writing styles and expressions.

3. The written summary is practised on modern domestic literature and a narrative of one's own is written.

4. In a discussion, students practise developing different points of view for a topic, which are justified with arguments. They also practise comparing, sorting, rating and summing up arguments in order to be able to make recommendations for or against an action.

5. Two works of authorship are created by the whole course. On the one hand, a book of fiction is written and then a feature film is made based on it.

6. Two works of authorship will be created by the entire course. On the one hand, a non-fiction book in the form of an anthology of scientific contributions will be produced and a documentary film will be made based on it.

9.15.2.3 Sport[122]

The physical education classes are divided into indoor sports, which are offered especially in winter, and outdoor sports, some of which only take place in summer. A certificate can always be obtained as soon as 2 sports have been learned and audited. If all 6 certificates are to be acquired, 12 out of 15 sports must be selected.

In winter, handball, hockey, gymnastics, badminton, swimming, winter sports and strength training are offered. In summer, football, street hockey, athletics, volleyball, basketball, climbing, jogging and cycling are offered.

9.15.2.4 Economy

Learners can invite a worker from a company in each course to interview them on the respective topics and get first-hand information. The Labour Directory is used to select the enterprises to be visited. Depending on the curriculum, small, medium or large family-owned, partner-owned or shareholder-owned businesses from different sectors are selected. Learners select the possible visitors through their profile in the Labour Directory to whom they would like to send a visit request. This may result in either a rejection, a class visit or an invitation to visit the company in question. All acceptances are voted on collectively by the course committee.

1.   Economic accounting to run a household frugally, balanced or wastefully in different income levels and living situations is practised. The use of the Labour Directory for purposes of consumption, accounting and finding work as an employee is practised.

2.   The learners carry out an imaginary business start-up in the 4 economic forms, including the preparation of market analyses of supply and demand, as well as the calculation of market entry costs through operation, personnel and business taxes.

3.   Learners run an imaginary company in the 4 economic forms including occupational safety and health,

---

122§184.2 Promotion of music, sport, film, culture and art: BV Art.68

profit functions, supply chains and insolvency.

4.	Learners practise how to turn savings into investments, through the People's Bank account[123] and other financial service providers, including stock market play on all domestic and international stock exchanges with all asset classes.

5.	Learners gain a deeper insight into the patent system by learning how patent examiners work and reenacting patent searches and patent examinations at an abbreviated level.

6.	Learners jointly set up a company of their election, preferably a business idea from a learner's idea diary. They run it for the duration of the course to obtain a certificate. If none of the learners wants to continue running the company, it will be closed again at the end of the course.

9.15.2.5 Music[124]

1.	Reading music is learned, as is the handling of classical musical instruments.

2.	Writing notes is learnt and the use of classical musical instruments to play according to notes.

3.	The handling of open-source computer programmes for music creation is practised, including the composition of a song consisting of bar, melody and song.

4.	Learners practise making music with their own bodies by humming, beatboxing, whistling, clapping, stamping, chest tapping and singing songs with or without karaoke.

5.	Learners dance to a wide variety of music and practise the classical dance steps, such as waltz, disco fox, samba or similar, which a teacher can offer.

6.	The course produces a piece of music and develops a choreography for it, which is danced by the learners for the accompanying music video.

---

123 Ministry of Finance - 11 People's Bank
124 §184.1 Promotion of music, sport, film, culture and art: BV Art.67a

9.15.2.6 Computer Science

Only open-source operating systems and programmes may be used in computer science lessons. For the introduction, learning programmes are used with which the learners learn the basic principles in programming and the structure of operating systems and programmes. Different programming languages can be tested within projects.

1.	In the Linux operating system, the handling of the open source software for creating texts, presentations and spreadsheets is practised.

2.	The programme Blender is used to create CAD models and 3D animations and to edit films.

3.	The complete programming of an application programming interface[125] as well as the partial programming of a website, programme or operating system is practised with the help of current open source software that the teacher has mastered.

4.	Any open source programme is to be extended or modified by own programming.

5.	The open source operating system is to be adapted to one's own wishes by changing the source code.

6.	A programme for a smartphone or computer is written by the whole course in a division of labour. This can also be a computer game. If functioning solar-powered computer kits come from the physics lessons, they are programmed as a priority and used to test new operating systems.

9.15.2.7 Chemistry

In the theory phase, the students choose which guest from the chemical industry will visit them or to which chemical factory a field trip will be made. In the practical phase, companies can choose products that are produced in class. All other products are produced only as prototypes in simple design or small quantities.

1.	Learners receive an introduction to the periodic table

---

125 Ministry of Digital - 12.5 Application Programming Interface for all directories

of the elements, the atomic model, the states of matter and Ph values of acids and bases.

2.	The current state of inorganic chemistry, which produces artificial things or artificially recreates natural things, is tested in experiments and prototypes.

3.	Acids, alkalis and gases are produced by electrolysis and other processes to sulphuric acid, soda ash, saltpetre, sodium carbonate and hydrogen.

4.	The current state of organic chemistry, which uses natural chemical processes for carbon-based metabolism, is tested in experiments and prototypes.

5.	Industrial goods such as synthetic fibres for composites or textiles, plastics, rubber, building materials such as cement, plaster or insulating and sealing agents are produced and, if possible, supplied to companies as remunerated contract work.

6.	Household products such as alcohol, soap, paint, paper, glue, gelatine, cosmetics, preservatives and chemical drugs are produced and tested. Chemical drugs are produced according to the purity law, but are only voluntary tested by age of majority.

9.15.2.8 Physics

In physics, learners are expected to make electricity, light, power and computers by being supplied with prefabricated assembly sets that are used to apply theoretical physics in experimental physics. The construction kits vary somewhat across the country. There are several variants with different technologies that learners are allowed to choose from. If possible, they come from companies and are assembled on their orders. The other construction kits are donations in kind that industry associations solicit from their companies. If too few donations are collected, the construction kits are financed through child benefits. If possible, employees of the industry from which the construction kit comes visit the classes.

1.	The mechanics include a single-seater automobile in the construction kit, which could be described as a mixture of soapbox and pedal car. These vehicles are used to race between all the surrounding schools.

2.	In the electricity lesson, there is a solar-powered computer in the construction kit, which could be described as a cross between a laptop and a smartphone. These computers are programmed in the computer science subject.

3.	In optics and acoustics, the construction kit consists of a video camera with manual adjustment options for focus, brightness and proximity, a light for flooding and spotting, and a microphone. The camera equipment is used for video production at the comprehensive school and is dismantled, maintained and cleaned before the end of the course.

4.	In thermodynamics, a power plant is in a construction kit that can be used to generate heat and electricity. The construction kits range from solar power plants to gas power plants to zeolite power plants and heat pumps. The power plants are used to generate electricity in the educational institution, the surplus of which can be fed into the public electricity network.

5.	In radio wave teaching, the assembly set includes a remote control and a receiver part that can be docked onto all computer-controlled assembly sets from the construction kits. Depending on the needs of the educational institution, an Internet-enabled school computer or Virtual Reality glasses are supplied here as an assembly set.

6.	In the physics of atoms, nuclei and quanta, an assembly set for a miniature magnetic resonance tomograph is being put together, which can be used to X-ray things the size of a mouse. Instead of an MRI, another analytical device can also be supplied that can contribute to basic research.[126]

9.15.2.9 Biology[127]

1.	Plants and ecosystems is the umbrella term under which learners grow, cross-breed, care for, cut up, eat or process agricultural crops in the school garden. The ecosystem in the school garden is inherently stabilised through permaculture to reduce human intervention. The harvest is processed and served in the canteen.

126§183.6 Research and innovation
127§220,3f Agriculture: BV Art.104

2.   Animals and territories are the theme that is reflected in the rearing of chickens at school. There is a chicken coop in the school garden that is looked after by the learners in this course all year round. Each learner can hatch a chick as part of the course and take it home. Remaining eggs are processed in the canteen, at least one egg must be hatched for the class. For each egg hatched, one adult chicken must be killed. The killed chicken is dissected and microscoped in the cell biology class and the edible parts are used in the canteen.

3.   The topic of behavioural biology and evolution is observed in the breeding and crossing of plants and chickens in the school garden. A family tree of the chickens and plants in the school garden is created using photos and leaves or feathers. Each learner logs and interprets the behaviour of a chicken or plant in the context of behavioural biology and compares their result with the logs of previous graduates of the course of relatives of the currently observed chicken.

4.   In cell biology, learners microscope and describe plant and animal cells and cell structures. Plants and feathers, raw eggs and raw meat from a chicken come from the school garden.

5.   In human biology, learners microscope human cells from hair, skin flakes, saliva, nasal mucus, sperm and menstrual blood. If an egg is discovered, artificial insemination is to be tried.

6.   Biotechnology is used for the topic of genetics and heredity. The biology lab has a bioreactor and a biocatalyst for this purpose. Biological principles of action are imitated in the bioreactor using examples of gene transfer and cell fusion, for example penicillin is produced. In a biocatalyst, enzymes, bacteria or fungi convert substances that are used in industrial production. In the biocatalyst, waste water is processed into drinking water and in the bioreactor, yeast is produced for further processing into bread and beer. The yeast is made available to the crafts to bake bread or brew beer.

9.15.2.10 Geography[128]

1.   Physical geography teaches the structure of the earth with continents, oceans, the interior of the earth, the earth's mantle, the earth's atmosphere and outer space, as well as the interaction that makes up the weather.

2.   By visiting mines, the teachers teach how mineral resources are searched for and extracted, for example iron for mechanical engineering, sulphur for chemistry or fertile soil for agriculture and the production of terra preta.

3.   The relationship between humans and the environment is explored in the consumption and processing of raw materials, as well as the effect of carbon dioxide and methane in a small airtight greenhouse.

4.   Each comprehensive school has a waste processing plant that can process the most current commodities so that they can be further processed. Learners in this course look after the waste processing plant all year round.

5.   Human geography is about human settlement on earth, national borders, cities and the migration of humans and vegetation.

6.   For one year, each student creates a movement pattern of him/herself. The results are continuously evaluated in the course. In the first half of the year, the means of transport are compared. The aim is to find out which is the most efficient means of transport for the short distance up to 25km and the transport of one person travelling alone. The production and operating costs are measured in money and toxins released.

In the second semester, the properties where the students spend most of their time are compared. The running costs and their structural composition are to be compared, how much money they cost and how many toxins construction and operation emit. Learners use this data to create a price-performance ratio in their living space, which is shown on a map. As a class visit, real estate agents can be invited or their visit appointments can be accompanied.

128§220,3f Agriculture: BV Art.104

9.15.2.11 Technology

1. Learners build models of Lego technology that are above their age limit. After testing and checking the performance characteristics of the models, they are taken apart again. Each year, a different model is to be built from all the individual parts that meets the requirements of the Examinations Office, for example, taking a load of 5 kilograms and setting it down again one metre higher.

2. Learners assemble a 3D printer from a supplied construction kit. This assembly set can easily be extended with additional parts available at any hardware store. Learners experiment with different materials, print heads and their simultaneous use. As a final project, a specific model is printed, which is specified by the Examinations Office. Before the start of the next course, the 3D printer is disassembled again and sorted into the construction kit. Before that, the other courses are allowed to use the printer.

3. Learners build a CNC milling machine themselves and receive building instructions for it, to which they do not necessarily have to adhere, as well as a budget that is the same every year. Material sourcing and processing is the responsibility of the whole course. Only one mark is awarded for the finished CNC milling machine and how accurately it can shape different materials into a given form. One CNC milling machine always stays in the comprehensive school, the other is sold after the course. The Examinations Office may also set another technical product as an assignment instead of a CNC milling machine.

4. Machines and plant construction are explained using real examples in industry. First, several employees from different industries come to build and maintain factory plants. Afterwards, factory plants from 3 sectors are visited. As a performance record, students have to build their own idea for a new plant as a virtual 3D model, including the programming of digital control devices. For the programming, the subject computer science is asked for help or at least one participant has already acquired the second certificate in computer science.

5.   In practical mechanical and plant engineering, the learners are to select a plant from the archive of virtual 3D models of the fourth course and build it in miniature format. The functioning of the miniature model is rated.

6.   Learners build a technical model taken from one of their idea diaries or they choose a technical idea considered innovative from the invention lessons. The functioning of the model is rated.

9.15.2.12 Crafts[129]

1.   All crafts related to food are covered, which includes the year-round care of the school garden. In the school garden, ridge beds are cultivated and harvested with vegetables and grain, and fish farming and a chicken coop are carried out, which counts as agriculture. The learners act as bakers when they grind grain from the school garden and bake bread from it, as butchers when they slaughter a chicken and make sausage from it, and as cooks when they prepare as many meals as possible in the school canteen from the food produced in the course.

2.   All crafts involved in clothing and design are covered. Hemp and linen are grown in the school garden and processed into coloured textiles. The handling of machines for weaving, knitting and sewing is practised, patterns are made and different textiles are processed into a clothing collection that the course creates and presents together.

3.   All crafts involved in raw materials, their extraction and processing are covered. Learners cut wood in a state forest and saw it into shapes, which the subject of house construction orders. They extract different types of stone to make building materials, which the subject of house construction orders.

4.   All crafts involved in metal and electrical processing are covered. As a mechanic, learners repair and test a mechanical tool, as an electronics technician a digital industrial machine, as a mechatronics technician a self-driving vehicle. This course is responsible for repairing and maintaining the machines

---

129§220.3f Agriculture: BV Art.104, §226.1 Housing and home ownership promotion: BV Art. 108

from the subjects of technology and physics.

5.   All crafts involved in chemical products are covered here. Learners make glass, paper, plastics, adhesives and solvents and can work with engineering, physics and chemistry subjects to do so.

6.   All crafts that serve the health of humans are covered here. The learners do each other's hair, care for nails, make dentures, hearing aids or glasses.

9.15.2.13 Policy

1.   Learners engage in family politics by creating and running a simulation game in which the roles of parents, siblings, relatives, friends and neighbours are assigned, who follows which patterns of action, what crises can arise and how to deal with them.

2.   Learners conduct enterprise policy by developing a simulation game. They assign roles to learners representing a trade association, a labour union and the Ministry of Labour to conduct collective bargaining. Times of crisis, such as bankruptcies, unemployment, labour shortages, as well as a boom are rehearsed.[130]

3.   Learners engage in municipal policy by controlling the municipal bodies of the ministries, simulating a budget vote for their municipality and creating a petition or initiative and trying to get the quorum to trigger it. During the holidays, learners have to do a two-week internship in a ministry other than the Ministry of Education.[131]

4.   Learners simulate national policy in a simulation game. They conduct elections of persons and legislative processes in the three variants of direct, indirect and representative form, including subsidiarity voting and counter-proposal by the party council. They limit the legislative process to the cooperation of at least 2 and at most 4 ministries. The ministry

130 Ministry of Labour - 16.8 Democratic collective bargaining, 14.7 Economic development, 14.9 Insolvency, Ministry of Finance - 7.5 Balancing the business cycle

131 Ministry of State Organisation - 11.5 Municipal policy, 9.10.11.7 Citizens' initiative, 9.10.11.6 Petition, 9.5 Quorum, Ministry of Finance - 9.5 Budget vote.

and the subject of the legislative initiative are chosen by the learners themselves. During the duration of this course, all learners must have a trial membership of 6 months in a party other than the Education Party.[132]

5.   Learners simulate supranational politics in a simulation game. They conduct accession negotiations for the outer ring of an international union and communitarise a ministry between at least 3 states in the middle ring and communitarise at least 2 constitutions of states establishing a federal state in the inner ring.[133]

6.   Learners simulate municipal, national and international responsibility for government in at least 2 ministries in a simulation game. In this simulation game, sudden crisis scenarios are given, such as social unrest, natural disasters, war, famine or pandemics. The policy decisions are simulated via the Algoracle[134] and the success or failure of government action is rated.[135]

9.15.2.14 History

In the history lessons about the epochs, tent camps are set up on the school grounds where learners in groups of 4 are supposed to live for 3 days one after the other. The time of year is decided by the learners in a course committee. Each educational institution has a camp with props that learners should assign to the appropriate period and use. It is possible to set up camps of all four epochs inside or outside the school grounds during the holidays.

In courses 1 to 4, the learners learn how humans lived in the respective epoch and prepare the tent camp and are given different challenges by the teacher, such as an attack by animals, drought, flood, diseases or war. Decider scenarios are re-enacted in the tent camp as an outdoor theatre.

1.   Stone Age

132 Ministry of State Organisation - 9.9 Election of persons, 9.10 Legislation, 9.8 State governments, 10.3 Subsidiary voting
133 Ministry of Foreign Affairs - 5.8 International Union
134 Ministry of Digital Affairs - 15.3 Algoracle
135 Ministry of State Organisation - 9.8 State Governments, 11 Federalism, 12 State Security

2. Ancient
3. Middle Ages
4. Modern times
5. The learners learn which world empires existed, which wars they waged, which peoples and mass murders or massacres they committed in order to become or remain a world empire.
6. Learners learn which revolutions have led to the overthrow of empires or national dictatorships and which innovations have decisively advanced certain eras.

9.15.2.15 Psychology

Permanent homework in the psychology subject in courses 1 and 2 is to keep a diary. The fields for experience and behaviour are listed in a table. This diary serves as a self-experiment and a visual object of one's own psyche.

For the whole subject, entries from anonymised diaries of the course participants serve as sample material for the learners. The psychological theories are explained with this sample material by the teacher. A general confidentiality about all details is agreed upon. Anyone who violates this will immediately be expelled from school.

1. Learners learn how humans experience their lives and how perception, memory, knowledge, thinking, problem solving, language and language comprehension differ for each human. Using the diary, learners explore themselves and others by writing down and sharing perceptions, thoughts, feelings, wishes and memories.

2. Learners experience how humans behave and how learning, emotion, motivation and action control are similar in every human. The diary is used to observe and communicate social action, communication and problem solving.

3. Developmental psychology teaches how early childhood development and changes in the experience and behaviour of humans can determine a human's life through punctual or protracted events and can beneficially or detrimentally influence the development of certain abilities and functions in social interaction. Learners describe their most moving

events in their own lives and observe their own development during the course. Each learner sets a goal at the beginning of the course, the gradual achievement or failure of which is recorded by the end of the course itself.

4.   In neurology, the study of the senses shows anatomically how our sensory organs take in stimuli, transport them along the nerve pathways to the brain, and there sort them into the developed pattern. Learners do self-experiments through training in which muscles are made to tense and relax with electricity, fear can be deliberately induced through a horror film or hilarity through a comedy. Sensory motor skills are practised in a massage circle.

5.   In social psychology, relationships between 2 or more persons and their effects on one's own experience and behaviour are analysed. During the course, learners keep a relationship log. Anonymised protocols of the following types of relationships are made: Couple relationship, Parent-child relationships, Grandparent-child relationships, Employer-employee relationship and Citizen-state relationship. As an examination, a play is performed in which each student has to embody given role patterns. The auditor must recognise all role patterns in order to achieve a grade of 1.

6.   Personality research looks at personal differences of all kinds, but especially appearance, milieu, age or gender and their influences on a person's perception and intelligence as a human. Each learner takes an IQ test at the beginning and end of the course. Between the two tests, mental exercises are given as homework. In class, learners practise researching the personalities of their fellow students, making predictions and then having the other person check them for accuracy. To do this, everyone looks for a partner, if necessary there may be a group of three. The partners may only be swapped once, provided that a swap partner can be found.

9.15.2.16 Ethics

In the subject ethics, regular church services are attended in the first and second seminar as a performance record. The sermons and contents are recorded in order to report to the learners in class. All church services in the area are regularly attended by the students in turn, so that a different student is present at each service and not always the same one. The minutes are forwarded by the teachers to the Integration Agency staff.[136]

1. Students learn about Christianity with its Protestant, Catholic and Orthodox denominations and Islam with its Sunni, Shia, Alevi and Judaism. Learners attend masses of all religions. Preachers may be invited into the classroom for a lesson.

2. Course participants learn about Hinduism and Buddhism with its Theravada, Mahayana and Vajrayana faiths. They get an overview of sects and what distinguishes them from the world religions.

3. The religious history of the country is taught to learners through local traditional religion and domestic virtues, manners and customs. Learners visit historical sites and invite grandparents to learn about domestic virtues, manners and customs.

4. In Constitutional Studies, learners find out more about the morality behind the domestic constitution. They visit the Constitutional Court and receive classroom visits from judges.

5. The most important ethical insights of Kant, Hegel, Schopenhauer and Nietzsche are taught to the learners and adapted for today's time.

6. The most significant ethical insights of Horkheimer, Adorno, Habermas and Kohlberg are taught to the learners and adapted for today.

136Ministry of Integration - 5.2 Field service

9.15.2.17 Languages

Language classes are offered in at least three languages. Each educational institution makes it dependent on the qualifications of the teachers whether English, German, French, Spanish, Russian or Chinese can be offered. Because everyone learns languages at different rates, there are no 6 different certificates, but the longer you attend language classes, the higher your language level rises, from basic knowledge to fluency to business fluency.

Vocabulary is practised with the oral exam helmets or the school computers. A query software supports the learners and saves the time of use and the results, vocabulary tests are thus replaced. Learners bring in audio plays, literature and videos or films and choose in a course committee which works will be covered in class. In class, radio plays, literature and videos are translated from the foreign language into the mother tongue. Afterwards, they talk about these stories or documentaries in the foreign language. In a course committee, one of the translated radio plays or videos is used to set it to music either in the national language or in the foreign language. Learners are given speaking parts for the respective actors. As an exam, learners produce their own stories or documentaries in the foreign language. For each language class, exchanges abroad are held once a year during the holidays with partner schools in the relevant country.

9.15.2.18 Art[137]

1. Learners make toys out of paper and wood.
2. Learners make toys out of metal and electronics
3. Learners create an animated film, among other things with specially made models from the first and second course.
4. Learners paint and draw with different tools and colours on different surfaces.
5. Learners create a cartoon or redesign walls and facades in the educational institution or municipality.
6. Students learn about the different building styles,

137§184.5 Promotion of music, sport, film, culture and art: BV Art.69

design a building of their election and make a model for it.

9.16 Foreign exchange

To strengthen international and continental cooperation, exchange programmes take place between cities in different countries. One-week stays abroad are organised between comprehensive schools in inland cities and schools in foreign partner cities. The pupils live alternately but not simultaneously with the host family and attend the host educational institution together. Participation in an exchange abroad is voluntary and only compulsory once in the foreign language learners are taking.

9.17 Student exchange

Between comprehensive schools within the country, learners should do a one-week exchange. In the case of domestic partner schools, it is important that they make cultural experiences possible. Therefore, if possible, partner schools should be located in different economic forms, educationally deprived or highly educated populations, neighbourhoods or cities with poorer and richer inhabitants, or inside or outside cultural protection areas. Both exchange partners get to know different ways of life in a country as well as a different family, friendly and neighbourly environment. The pupils live alternately but not simultaneously with the host family. The student exchange is voluntary and only compulsory once for the subject Integration.

9.18 Final years 11 to 13

During the final years, the learning content of the previous 6 learning years is repeated and further deepened. Learners must decide before the start of the 11th learning year in which subjects they would like to complete their degree. Only the content of these subjects is repeated in the 11th learning year and is further deepened and examined in the 12th and 13th learning years. Instead of the central performance record, all learners aiming for a higher educational qualification also take part in the final examinations.

Learners who only want to take the basic qualification leave the comprehensive school after the 11th year. Learners who only want to take the advanced qualification leave the comprehensive school after the 12th year. Students who wish to take the college entrance qualification leave the comprehensive school after the 13th year.

The teaching in the final years of the selected subjects is composed of consolidations of the learning years 5 to 10, which have their focus on theory, and goes as far beyond the material up to the 10th learning year as is necessary to be at university level after the 13th learning year.

Since every citizen has the right to go back to the comprehensive school at any time to catch up on a degree, older learners are also in the courses, especially in the last three years.

9.19 Final examinations[138]

The Ministry of Education determines the contents of the final examinations in voting with the Ministries of Labour, Economy and Innovation.[139] Compulsory subjects in all qualifications are the national language, one "technical" subject and a foreign language. Performance subjects have twice the number of hours per week and deepen the content even further. The examination questions for performance subjects are correspondingly more difficult. In the comprehensive school, "technical" subjects mean maths, biology, physics, chemistry, technology, computer science and crafts. By general education subjects, all subjects are meant, except "technical" subjects.

---

138 §176.4 Education space
139 Ministry of Labour - 11.2.1 Necessary educational content

9.19.1 Basic qualification

For the basic qualification, learners must take the crafts subject and the Examinations Office conducts a project exam in this subject. Learners aiming for a higher educational qualification who have not taken craftsperson must participate in project teaching in a "technical" subject in the 11th learning year and have this project rated.

9.19.2 Advanced qualification

For the advanced qualification, learners select one foreign language and 3 additional subjects of their choice. From these 6 subjects, learners must choose a performance subject. In the examination, one subject must be examined by a presentation, which corresponds to a combination of written and oral exam.

9.19.3 College entrance qualification

For the college entrance qualification, 2 foreign languages, a freely selectable "technical" subject, a freely selectable general education subject and a completely freely selectable subject are chosen. From these 7 subjects, learners must choose 2 performance subjects. The 7 examinations must be conducted using a written, oral or project-based examination method. The examinees themselves decide in which subject they want to be examined with which method.

9.19.4 Examination method

Which subject is examined in which way is usually left up to the students. There is a choice of written, oral or project-oriented exams. Which tasks are set is left to the Examinations Office. The recording of performance is left to the examining teachers. The same applies here as in all other central performance records: Other teachers must correct written exams or take the oral or project exams. The auditors must not know the examinees. The aim is for examinees to stand on their own two feet and make a first impression that will be received impartially by the auditors. In each final examination, the report marks of the previous two school years count towards the final mark.

9.19.5 Examination procedure

Written exams last 2 hours in the basic subject and 4 hours in the performance subject. Oral exams last 30 minutes in the basic subject and 60 minutes in the performance subject, of which half as much time is additionally granted as preparation time beforehand. During the examination period, the examinee gives a lecture for half of the examination time and answers questions from the auditors for the other half. Project exams last 30 minutes, in addition to the examination of the written papers. Presentation examinations last 30 minutes, with 15 minutes divided between the examinee's presentation and 15 minutes for answering questions. In addition, the presentation is examined with a written paper.

9.19.6 Examination period

The exams for the lower secondary and advanced qualifications as well as the college entrance qualification are taken at the end of the school year, i.e. in the middle of the summer holidays over several weeks. At the beginning of the new school year, the graduates are then allowed to celebrate one school day at the school. This celebration should also be the welcome party for the new fifth graders.

9.19.7 Repeating final examinations

As soon as the average of all final examinations is more than 4.0, the degree must be repeated. The repetition of individual examinations of individual subjects is not possible. All final examinations of the comprehensive school that have not been passed can be repeated 3 times within 5 years.

The exception is the basic qualification, which can be repeated any number of times. It does not have to be repeated because school attendance is no longer compulsory. If you do not pass the basic qualification, you have two more attempts. If you do not pass any of the three attempts, you can repeat the 11th learning year at the special school as often as you like and try for the basic qualification.

For learners who aspire to a higher qualification but already fail at the one below, they must first achieve that qualification before they are allowed to progress to the next final year.

10 People's Service[140]

People's Service must be completed by all genders after graduation from comprehensive school. People's Service lasts one year and can be divided into a maximum of four parts. The first compulsory quarter is basic training[141] for the military and the People's Protection Service. The remaining three quarters can be completed in different institutions or in the same institution. People's Service can be done in the Social Village[142], Non-profit Companies[143], Non-profit Institutions[144], Construction Team[145], People's Protection Service[146], State Hospitals[147] or University Hospitals[148]. The year groups are trained during the holidays between the tenth and eleventh learning year in the nearest Social Village.

During the People's Service, a monthly wage equal to the child

---

140 §174 Military and People's Service: BV Art. 59
141 Ministry of Security - 9.4.1 Basic Training
142 Ministry of Planned Economy - 17.1 Social welfare
143 Ministry of Social Market Economy - 11.2 Non-profit companies
144 Ministry of Family Affairs - 9.7 Honorary service
145 Ministry of Infrastructure - 5.8 Construction Team
146 Ministry of Security - 6 People's Protection Service
147 Ministry of Planned Economy - 18.1.3 Health Centre
148 Ministry of Health - 5.6.1 University Hospitals

benefit is paid. Housing in a Social Village is only available if the accommodation is not provided by the beneficiary or by the family. This may apply in exceptional cases. The rule during a period of national service for which a move is necessary is to stay with state employees in their guest rooms, in barracks, Social Villages or construction workers' housing provided by the Ministry of Infrastructure.

People's Service workers are deployed in such a way that they can stay with their parents if possible, apart from basic training. However, since there is freedom of choice for 9 months of the 12 months as to which posts People's Service workers can apply to, posts close to home are to be accepted first. Three posts must be selected for the application, which will be ranked. Unpopular but necessary posts will be filled by lottery. A working day of a minimum of 8 hours and a maximum of 12 hours applies. The hourly wage rate is the same as the Social Market Economy minimum wage. The low wage is justified by the fact that this work performance for the state community is in return for the training received free of charge during the school career.

11 College[149]

Colleges, vocational training colleges and universities are the educational institutions responsible for study, teaching, academic career paths and continuing education. The vocational training colleges are responsible for vocational education, the universities for scientific education. The state vocational training colleges, colleges and universities are all run with the same democratic structures and processes as all other educational institutions.

Colleges are educational institutions that provide scientific education by conducting teaching and research at the highest level of education. The vocational training colleges provide vocational education but also participate in research, thus providing an interface between theoretical and practical research. The vocational training colleges collect data during their training in the companies, which the vocational training colleges collect through their work assignments and use for

149 §180.4 Schools and colleges: BV Art. 63a

research purposes at the colleges. Due to this fact, all work done by the vocational training college students should meet scientific requirements by citing or quoting all sources used.

On the one hand, the aim of colleges is to provide students with a universal understanding of the world and a profound understanding of the subject, so that they can work in several appeals in one field. On the other hand, colleges aim to employ the broadest possible team of researchers. These researchers conduct research for municipal and national government, the people, and for the Planned Economy and Social Market Economy.

In contrast to universities, colleges are not bound by state requirements to cover certain research areas or to conduct contract research for the ministries. In individual cases, however, a research community can be formed from all colleges with corresponding subject areas after a referendum. Unlike universities, colleges do not have to have all subject areas.

The funding of vocational training colleges, colleges and universities can be different. While vocational training colleges can claim contributions from the industry associations for which they provide training, universities are entirely Tax-funded in order to be as independent as possible. Colleges can establish institutes with which they offer fee-based and profit-making services.

In the following, the term college is used for colleges, vocational training colleges and universities. Vocational training colleges and universities are only mentioned if different conditions apply to them.

11.1 Subject areas

Colleges represent the totality of all subject areas. The subject areas are differentiated into the various sciences found in the different educational institutions. Teachers for a subject area are trained in it at the colleges. This means subject areas range from basics that are already found in all nursery schools to specialist departments that are only found at individual colleges.

11.2 University

Universities are those colleges that have all subject areas. Universities also house the research institutes of the ministries. Universities thus directly serve the people by providing specialised personnel to advise or inform the ministries and provide information to their fellow citizens on committees as recognised informed citizens with detailed knowledge of causes and effects. At least one university is located in each capital city of a ministry.

Universities have stricter selection criteria for their students and academic staff. Universities maintain close contact with colleges, care for exchange programmes with students from colleges and have visiting lecturers from colleges. Where a university is ordered to do so by a ministry or committee, it must give priority to the tasks ordered. For this purpose, universities may also require all members of all state colleges to serve. The purpose of universities is to facilitate admission of the wealth of knowledge and scholars of the Ministry of Education to other ministries and the people. Universities have the sovereign task of strengthening the security and innovative power of the people.

11.3 Vocational training college[150]

At the vocational training college, all vocational training courses are offered that constitute in-service training for craftspersons. The ministries of labour, economy and innovation decide on the learning content together with the Ministry of Education when drawing up the curriculum. Educational institutions coordinate with companies and adapt the curriculum to the training situations. The vocational training college can be part of a college or an independent educational institution. Learners put together their own timetable and choose their own teachers. While at the vocational training college and in a company learning the crafts in practice, one is considered an apprentice. In a training company, a master's craftsperson must train the apprentice. At the vocational training college,

---

150§181,1,3 Vocational education and training: BV Art. 63

teachers train the apprentices theoretically. After graduation, you are considered a journeyman. You can become a master's craftsperson after 3 years of work experience as a journeyman and further in-depth studies at the vocational training college.

11.4 Free time at the college

Between courses, learners can play games and do sports on the university grounds, the So-called campus. On an outdoor court, playing fields are recorded where ludo can be played with humans as pieces or a chess board for which pieces can be lent out. Game materials and sports equipment can be lent out in the library. Headphones and radio frequency transmitters can be lent out for a headphone party so that people can dance with each other on campus. When waiting outside an office, games are available for people waiting to play together, such as a miniature skittles game with a marble as a bowling ball.

In summer and winter, a party is held at the end of the semester. It is hosted by the students and takes place in all lecture halls and seminar rooms, except for laboratories and rooms with machines. Everything should be as open as possible. In case of damage to property, cameras must be installed for the party next time. The recordings from these cameras can be used by volunteers free of charge for video editing for promotional purposes. Student councils can organise parties at any time outside the opening hours of the educational institution for which they are responsible.

11.5 College and Educational Television[151]

The Ministry of Media Affairs, in cooperation with the Ministry of Education, organises the filming of knowledge taught at state educational institutions. The educational institutions cooperate with the Educational Television[152] , which is responsible for the technical executive. The content is determined by the teachers in voting with the Examinations

---

151 §184.3 Promotion of music, sport, film, culture and art: BV Art.71
152 Ministry of Media - 13 Educational Television

Office. Learners make these films in whole or in part in their performance records or final papers. Teaching videos for the learning content of the nursery school, primary school and comprehensive school are made by learners who are studying to become teachers. Textbooks and anthologies of professional literature are used as source material for the screenplays. The educational videos can be created as a documentary, feature film or show. Educational Television assists with implementation by providing editorial advice, technical equipment and training, as well as studios, film sets and actors. The finished videos are broadcast on Educational Television and from then on are stored in the Knowledge Directory under the corresponding course.

The aim is for citizens to be able to inform themselves about all educational content, both to learn and to control whether the Ministry of Education is spending taxpayers' money wisely.

11.6 Teaching

Teaching at vocational training colleges, colleges and universities takes place within subject areas and is called study. Each subject area has a teachers' council and a student council. The duration of a study programme depends on the performance and learning success of the students. Basically, a learning year consists of two semesters of classes and there are holidays between the two semesters. Usually, performance records and final examinations take place during the holidays. The area on which a college is located is called a campus. It is possible for a college to have several campuses in one city.

The certificates are divided into performance certificates and seat certificates. Performance certificates replace the central performance records. The contents of the lessons and the performance records are determined by each subject area. The way in which the lessons and the performance record are delivered is determined by the teacher.

11.6.1 Application

If you want to study at a state educational institution, you have to go through an application run-through. The election of subjects, location and application are done digitally through the Education Directory.

11.6.1.1 Choice of subjects

In the Education Directory, you select the subjects you would like to study. By linking to the Labour Directory, vacancies requiring that subject as a degree are displayed. There is a green circle with a number in it, i.e. the number of vacancies of domestic companies from all four economic forms. If you click on the green circle, all companies are displayed on a map. Clicking on a company takes you to that company's profile page in the Labour Directory.

11.6.1.2 Selection of the study location

To select the educational institution, you are shown where the desired subjects are offered in the vicinity or you enter one or more locations yourself. The course lists can be accessed in the Education Directory via the group of the binding institution. There, a subject area is selected to access the course list. From the course list, one selects a specific course in this subject because one likes the description of the course and reports for a course. You repeat the same procedure for all courses that interest you, regardless of the subject area. One attends at least one session in a course from each subject area for the major and minor. The teacher confirms the attendance in the Education Directory. The aim is to create a timetable for a trial week. Students who are still at the comprehensive school must schedule the trial week during the comprehensive school holidays.

11.6.1.3 Application procedure

You apply for up to three fields of study, whereby rankings are assigned. You also have to state up to three specific career aspirations. If there are enough places available, you will receive your first choice. The educational institutions indicate how many places they have available and an algorithm shows applicants where they can study. From these, applicants select all those they like and send an application there. The application is automatically generated using the data from all the directories to create a CV including testimonials. An additional letter of motivation is only necessary if required by the educational institution.

The educational institutions make the selection criteria democratically as to which applicants they accept or reject. Once the maximum number of places has been reached, the basis for acceptances must be the final grade and the grades in the comprehensive school subjects corresponding to the desired fields of study. An average grade is calculated from these grades, which is called the numerus clausus. Those who only receive rejections can automatically apply for their second and third choice.

If you are accepted, you will receive a starter package. This tells you which degrees can be taken in this subject and which certificates you have to have taken by when for which degree.

11.6.1.4 Expansion

As soon as rejections occur, every application case whose initial wish could not be fulfilled is reported to the Education Authority. If no wish could be fulfilled and the numerus clausus had to serve as a benchmark, the case is also reported to the Education Authority. If an applicant who was once rejected has graduated in the first desired subject after a change of subject, a new report is made for this case. The case reports automatically trigger an application for an extension. If the motions pile up so that an expansion with new rooms and more teachers covers the costs per capita of students, the Education Authority sends a report to the Minister of

Education. Depending on the annual budget, extensions are implemented. The aim is to ensure that there is no shortage of knowledge that the population wants to learn. Referendums can concretise this aspiration and thus justify a rejection of the expansion of a college.

11.6.2 Acclimatisation phase

During the semester break, the new students are introduced to student life for a week by sponsors, i.e. students from the second semester onwards. During this week, first-year students are supposed to spend the night together if possible, either in a tent camp on campus or a dormitory in the lecture halls or with volunteers from the student dormitory. During this week, students are shown all the rooms on campus that are needed, especially secretariats and faculty workrooms.

11.6.3 First semester

In the first semester, a compulsory course is required in which an overview of the basics of the subject is given. You can only freely choose one course in which you can take a performance certificate. Seat certificates can always be taken. Attendance is compulsory for the compulsory course and is controlled by attendance lists. In the compulsory course, the learning content of a degree programme is taught within one semester. This is made possible by students from higher semesters sharing their summaries. Textbooks are summarised by students in the course of their studies, usually as part of a performance record. The teacher receives these texts. She chooses the most appropriate and shortest summary and then asks the students whether it is written in a comprehensible way. These summaries are published in an anthology, which is compulsory reading for students in the first semester. The compulsory course is completed with a performance record. If you pass, you receive the introductory certificate.

11.6.4 The following semesters

You can put together your own timetable in all subsequent semesters. This means that all courses that one has chosen from the course catalogue may be attended. Depending on which degree or degrees students choose, they collect all the prescribed certificates. There should be a choice of different courses for a certificate. Thus, one should not be forced to study a certain subject with a certain teacher. It is possible, however, that for certain courses prior knowledge is necessary, for which one must first have acquired certain certificates. This prior knowledge is already indicated in the course description of the course catalogue. The prior knowledge must be so varied that it cannot be acquired additionally during the course. If prior knowledge is presumed to be too high, students can report this to the Examinations Office and arrange for an examination, the result of which they must be informed of and report on. If they doubt the result, they can take the case to the Remit Courts for Education.

The teachers specify the rooms and times for the courses. In the first week, the participants who want to stay to do the certificates are identified. Now the rooms are changed if necessary so that there is enough space everywhere. Any student who has to sit on the floor due to lack of space can report to the Education Authority via the Education Directory. Attendance is not compulsory in the courses and there is no minimum number of hours to be completed per week. The only requirement is to pass the certificates required for graduation.

11.6.4.1 Performance certificates

Performance certificates consist of written exams, oral exams, presentations and assignments. Presentations are given in front of the teacher and course participants on a deadline date. For written exams and oral exams, knowledge is tested on an examination date. Assignments have a deadline.

11.6.4.2 Seat certificates

Students should get to know the whole college. They should look at every subject that even remotely interests them. These are the seat certificates. You don't have to take an exam, just go and listen or participate.

11.6.5 International students

There are always as many foreign students at the college as there are of its own students studying at foreign colleges. To this end, colleges set up continent-wide and international exchange programmes. All these matters are handled by the international secretariat at the colleges.

Students who study abroad can take all certificates there. They are either recognised as seat certificates or, if they fit the subject area, as performance certificates for a degree. You can also ask your own subject area about recognition beforehand.

11.6.6 Cleaning and catering

Students in the first two semesters have to do cleaning and catering duties at the college to save on staff costs and avoid elitist thinking among academics.

11.6.7 Sanctions

Anyone who disrupts the lecture will be sent out of the room by the teacher and may not appear again until the next course date.

Students who fail the same performance test three times must change their field of study or leave the college.

In case of poor survey results in different courses, teachers are transferred or dismissed unless they are excellent researchers. Such researchers are then no longer employed in teaching.

11.6.8 University degrees[153]

The Ministry of Education, in voting with the Ministries of Labour, Economy and Innovation, determines the different types of higher education degrees.[154] Different degrees are offered at different educational institutions. At vocational training colleges, the crafts degrees journeyman and master's craftsperson can be obtained. At colleges and universities, the academic degrees Bachelor, Master, Diploma and Master's Graduate can be obtained. Students can take certificates and opt for any degree at any time by registering for the examination, provided they can produce the necessary certificates. Depending on the degree, a different run-through must be taken. The Bachelor's and Master's degrees are internationally communitarised degrees to make it easier for students to change colleges or jobs between countries. Internships must be completed during all degree programmes. It is up to the students to decide whether the internships accompany their studies, take place during the semester break or whether they take a semester off.

11.6.8.1 Bachelor & Master

The Bachelor is the postgraduate course for the in-depth course called Master. The educational institution or country can be changed between or during the degree programmes. Those who wish to seamlessly add the Master to the Bachelor at the same educational institution do not have to newly apply. For the Bachelor and Master, the timetable is largely influenced by modules, which consist of several similar courses and must be passed one after the other. In addition, there are So-called Creditpoints (CP), i.e. points that are earned for passing a certificate. They depend on the scope of the learning content and the number of hours per week for a course. In most cases, the CP vary between 8 and 15 CP per certificate. 30 CP should be achieved per semester, which should correspond to 40 hours of work. 30 CP per semester is recommended in

---

153§176.4 Education space
154Ministry of Labour - 11.2.1 Necessary educational content

order to be able to meet the standard period of study, but is not obligatory. In addition to the CP, grades are awarded for the performance records. There are no seat certificates. The final grade is made up of the grades of all performance records and final examinations. In both degree programmes, at least 2 internships with a total duration of at least 4 months must be completed, which is confirmed by the employer through the work certificate.

The Bachelor's degree programme consists of a major subject and a minor subject. The standard period of study for this is 6 semesters. The Bachelor's thesis must be about 40 pages long and counts for 20% of the final grade.

The Master's degree programme consists of a major subject and 2 minor subjects. The standard period of study for this is 4 semesters. The Master's thesis must comprise about 60 pages and be defended in an oral exam. Both performances count for 40% of the final grade.

11.6.8.2 Diploma & Master's Graduate

The Diploma and Master's Graduate are two independent degree programmes, which are divided into basic studies and main studies. The basic study period ends after the 4th semester. The learning content and the performance records for the certificates become more extensive in the main study period. There is no examination between the basic and main studies, only a testimonial with all previous grades for the certificates acquired. Certificates from the main study period can also be acquired at the time of the basic study period, which allows students to freely arrange their timetables.

For the Diploma and Master's Graduate, there are subject areas from which a certain number of performance certificates must be acquired. Overlaps can occur, i.e. certificates can be used for several subject areas, but only submitted once. It is up to the student to decide which certificates to acquire and when. In addition, there is a prescribed number of seat certificates that must be acquired at other subject areas. Students who take part in the performance record for a seat certificate can also acquire the certificate and list it on their final testimonial.

Performance certificates only have to be passed. Grading takes place, but the grades are not included in the final grade. A performance record is considered passed up to a grade of 4. The final grade is made up of the grades of all final examinations. In both degree programmes, at least 4 internships with a total duration of at least 8 months must be completed, which is confirmed by the employer through the work certificate.

The diploma programme consists of a major subject and 3 minor subjects. The standard period of study for this is 12 semesters. The diploma thesis must be about 100 pages long and written or oral exams must be taken, one exam per minor subject and 2 exams per major subject. This results in the final grade.

The Master's degree programme consists of 2 main subjects. The standard period of study for this is 12 semesters. The Master's thesis must be about 100 pages long and 2 written or oral exams must be taken for each major subject. This results in the final grade.

11.6.9 Final testimonial

In the final testimonial, all grades of the final examinations and passed certificates are indicated with the title of the course, including seat certificates and voluntary performance certificates at foreign subject areas. The final testimonial is presented at a formal ceremony. The educational institutions determine the manner of the ceremony independently.

11.7 Research

Research serves to advance science. At state educational institutions, research is conducted on an ongoing basis by all members. To ensure equal opportunities, the Ministry of Education regulates the funding of research projects and the publication of research results in a uniform manner. The infrastructure extends from the central office in the Ministry of Education to the Examination Office and the Education Authority to all educational institutions that conduct research independently or in a joint research association. All state research belongs to the people because it is financed in whole or in part by tax revenue. Therefore, all research data must be available to all educational institutions simultaneously and published via the Knowledge Directory. For research data that is at risk of being pirated, separate protected areas will be created in the Knowledge Directory until the research results are protectable. Researchers who withhold research data are liable to prosecution. Those who denigrate researchers for their research data are liable to prosecution because they violate the freedom of research.

11.7.1 Research community

Research is carried out in the state-wide network of all state institutions. All research results are immediately entered in the Knowledge Directory. All research is supported by all institutions. For example, if psychologists develop a test to study moral development in youths, the experimental design is sent to all educational institutions and teachers interview their learners and send the results to the researchers. All quantitative and qualitative data collected in state agencies must be stored on the intranet. Through these data sets, state researchers have continuous access to a large data set for their specialist department. If a study is not possible with the existing data, researchers at state colleges and universities may ask other state employees to conduct the study on their clients. However, the data sets may only be transmitted anonymously. If this is not the case, the clients must be asked for permission beforehand. Researchers also have the option of sending requests to all users via the directories, but always with an indication of the purpose behind this survey. Anyone who deceives here is liable to prosecution.

11.7.2 State research institutes[155]

Scientific research institutes report to the respective ministry, such as the Institute of Occupational Health to the Ministry of Health. These research institutes consist of the scientific personnel of the state colleges. Salaries for foreign specialists must be expelled separately in the budget. The research institutes of the ministries can commission colleges with research projects that must be given priority. In return, however, additional funds flow from the ministry's institute to the college in question. This money must flow into the research budget of the scientists who worked for the state research project and had to put their own research on hold for it. As compensation, they receive the money from the ministry, which they can use to advance their own research. How exactly is at the discretion of the researchers.

The following control mechanisms are in place against research misconduct: Researchers at the state colleges can voice their scientific concerns when they see the publications on the intranet or learn about them from the media. If faults are suspected, university researchers are allowed to inspect and review the research protocols of the state institutes. If faults are found or inadequate research methods are used, an audit is carried out by all colleges with that subject area in which the ministry belongs. The legality auditors of the Company Auditing Agency are involved in these audits.[156]

11.7.3 Publications

For any publications by state educational institutions, all researchers involved must be listed by name, according to the total number of working hours on the research project that contributed to the publication.

155§183.2 Research and innovation: BV Art. 64
156Ministry of Labour - 20.7.6 Legality auditor

11.7.4 Research projects with companies[157]

The money for research projects is provided by the Ministry of Education or through the Research Cost Fund[158] . The motions for research projects come either from companies in the Barter Economy, Planned Economy and Social Market Economy or from researchers.

Entrepreneurs report to the Ministry of Education which research projects would help them to make technical progress in their companies, whether this concerns work processes or products. The innovation auditors of the Company Auditing Agency[159] are responsible for asking the companies about their research needs and forwarding them to the Ministry of Education. The Ministry of Education aggregates suitable proposals and reports them to the companies if a sufficient number of companies have the same research objective and communicates the aggregated proposals to the comprehensive schools and colleges. The educational institutions decide in voting with each other in the council of managers who can and would like to implement which research projects. The Education Authority is responsible for mediation and can force the implementation of a research project on behalf of the Minister of Education.

Professors, doctors, research assistants, students and pupils have the opportunity to submit proposals for research projects. The Research Directory with its interfaces to the Education Directory serves as an aid here. There, all proposals, whether from researchers or companies, can be named, discussed and rated in a group, including subgroups that can be freely created. It is also possible to bind proposals to an existing research project, to connect several similar research projects and to establish working groups across comprehensive schools and colleges.

Teachers can vote in the teachers' councils which research projects fit best into their teaching and research plans. These research projects are marked separately. The work share of the comprehensive school and college in the research project is

---

157 §183.6 Research and innovation
158 Ministry of Innovation - 5.3.1 Research Cost Fund
159 Ministry of Labour - 20.7.5 Innovation auditor

indicated. Depending on the budget situation of the Ministry of Education, more or fewer research projects are approved or rejected that cannot be financed through the Research Cost Fund. The orders financed by the state are decided by the Minister of Education, if savings from the Ministry of Education are to be spent on them, or by the people in the budget vote. However, if the savings are to be spent, a quorum of 30% can lead to all research projects for that year being published on the intranet and selected by the people in a voting process.

All proposals for research projects must receive ratings in the form of marks between 1 and 6. Ratings are to be given as to how curricular, cross-school, forward-looking for all mankind or business-friendly they are. For research projects that are to benefit individual entrepreneurs, the economic form in which the company or companies are registered must be indicated.

For example, costly basic research that brings in no revenue at all without specialised research can be outsourced to the pupils or students. They are expected to do this work when they take practical exams. The results from the highest graded papers nationwide are then evaluated by professional researchers from the colleges.

11.7.5 Policy advice

The Examinations Office continuously evaluates performance records and theses that have references to current policy debates and identifies the responsible student council and professorship. Ministries, political parties or committees that need expert advice can convene an academic advisory board, in which all voluntary learners can participate and teachers must attend. The student council sends the voluntary students with the highest marks in the subject and the subject area sends the teachers with the highest marks in the surveys and grade averages in the central performance records. The Examinations Office ensures that the academic teaching staff or voluntary selected students are placed with the ministries that need the expertise. Once the educated persons have been identified, they give their opinion on the state of research via video message on the intranet. Each college controls the embassy and rates it with grades from 1 to 6. Only users of the intranet who have at least a degree in the relevant subject are eligible for this rating. Comments can be written by all users of the Education Directory. The Ministry of Education is responsible for appointing members of an educational institution as academic advisors to committees and councils. The learners, teachers and researchers who are most well read in the subject in question throughout the country and who have received top marks or praise for it are appointed as advisory board members. In matters of early childhood education, voluntary children can also participate in the scientific advisory board if they can already speak and show commitment in the committees.

Even in science, there is rarely just one right way or the one true truth. Therefore, at least two learners, teachers and researchers each should participate in a policy advisory board. They act in an advisory capacity and have the same voting rights as any other citizen.

12 Free education[160]

Free admission to education is guaranteed at all times for nationals of employable age. Compulsory schooling applies to the qualification of adolescents, and there are various opportunities for further education for adults. Degrees can be obtained on the basis of any previous education. Skills acquired through certificates do not expire, but can be used for another qualification in the course of one's life.

12.1 Social Village boarding school

The educational institutions in the Social Villages are at the same time state boarding schools, where any citizen may graduate at any time. The prerequisite is that his place of residence is too far away from the appropriate educational institution and that he must attend real classes because his

---

160 §182,1,3 Further education: BV Art. 64a

performance in the virtual classes of digital education is not sufficient. Minors who do not want to live with their parents also go to this boarding school. Each minor is allowed to admit himself to the boarding school up to 3 times and then for at least one year.

12.2 Open educational institutions

Educational institutions should be accessible to every citizen, especially classes and examinations. In this way, everyone can easily catch up on qualifications or continue their education, whether voluntarily, as a measure for the unemployed, as an inventor or for those in employment at the request or order of their employer. In this way, young learners learn early on what lifelong learning means when clearly older humans are present in their classes during some hours. In this way, minors may make less nonsense and talk to humans with more life experience during breaks.

12.3 Adult Education Center (AEC)

The Adult Education Centre (AEC) is a school by citizens for citizens. Here, anyone can become a teacher and teach what they want. Anyone who wants to become a teacher at the AEC must register their activity with the Education Authority by submitting a course description and a fee request. The fee must cover at least the Social Market Economy minimum wage and state administrative expenses. The fee is transferred after each course. If a course is insufficiently attended so that the minimum fee cannot be paid, the course may no longer be offered as long as other teachers wish to offer other courses. The AEC's premises are educational institutions or state premises out of hours that are suitable for teaching. AEC teachers are lent keys to the premises or use their identity card as a digital key. The Education Authority arranges for easy admission to the premises.

All AEC courses can be booked by all intranet users via the Education Directory. All AEC teachers who jointly offer courses in an educational institution or location automatically establish a group. This group is the AEC intranet site through which content and dates for teaching events can be found out, booked and paid for. Anyone who is registered for a course may join the group and is given the opportunity to access shared forums and data.

As soon as there is a shortage of rooms, the distribution mechanism is regulated by the number of participants. Participants can vote through their bookings which course they would like to attend and only the most popular courses take place.

12.4 Digitised education[161]

The Ministry of Education, in cooperation with the Ministries of Media and Digital, is creating a self-learning programme called learning game[162] , which can be used to achieve any degree. It is a mixture of video game, telecollege, solving tasks in writing or mathematically on the PC and creating or processing things via motion detection camera and Virtual Reality glasses[163] . It is based on film footage from the film teams that are on the road in all educational submissions.

Since users do not take up human time and there is no cost for infrastructure, they can try each exam as many times as they want. The grades calculated by the programme are supposed to be slightly more difficult to achieve than in the real educational institution.

Every user who has completed all digital preliminary examinations with at least a grade 2 can register for the final examination in suitable educational institutions. Which educational institutions are suitable is automatically displayed to the user. The final examinations take place at the same time with the same examination tasks as for all learners at the educational institutions. They are also corrected and rated

---

161 §182.2 Further education: BV Art. 64a
162 Ministry of Digital Affairs - 15.8 Educational Game
163 Ministry of Digital Affairs - 13.6.9.1 Virtual reality glasses

by teachers and, if they pass, the examinees receive a final testimonial.

The learning game is accessible to all users in the Knowledge Directory when they order the appropriate Virtual Reality glasses and sensor clothing via the Knowledge Directory or purchase or lend out the glasses in the Intranet Café.

All prisons have specially secured computers through which prisoners can only log into the educational game and do all the practical parts with the sensor clothing. Prisoners cannot contact or see other users and avatars. This way, prisoners can use the off-duty time to be able to register for the final exam after detention.

12.4.1 Training glasses

The training glasses are intended for the performance of all kinds of work by laypersons. Various tasks are filmed so that the worker wearing Virtual Reality glasses can see them in front of his or her current background. Educational institutions, state enterprises, Planned Businesses and Planned Enterprises of the Planned Economy as well as voluntary companies of all economic forms digitise their work steps. The most successful work steps are automatically recognised and communicated to all participating companies. All recordings are stored in the Knowledge Directory and their quality can be rated by the users.

12.4.1.1 Example construction work

Construction workers get a pair of transparent Virtual Reality glasses with a barcode scanner, similar to google glass. All components have a barcode and the construction worker is shown in the glasses where the component is currently located and where it has to go. All the glasses are networked so that components can never be registered more than once and that the stock levels are registered. If persons without Virtual Reality glasses are also working, the construction site and the building materials warehouse must be filmed with a rotating camera on a drone at the beginning of a working day.

At the start of a construction worker's shift, a list is displayed as soon as the construction worker is in the building materials store. The glasses show: hole screwdriver size 5, 100 screws size 5, cordless screwdriver B, battery bb. The construction worker is shown the way with an arrow in the glasses. A red dot appears on the spot where the screwdriver is. The glasses scan the barcode and send to all the other glasses that this screwdriver is now gone and if it is to be accessed, the other glasses know which signal to locate in order to find the screwdriver and its current function. Arrows now appear in the worker's field of vision to guide him to his workstation. He can preview work steps and switch through stages in the architect's 3D drawing: A) finished building, B) current construction progress, C) next work step of this construction worker, D) daily target, E) weekly target. In case of problems, a competent person can switch on and see the video image of the glasses and talk to the construction worker.

12.5 Passive education

When buying and consuming products, information should be provided about the products, but also in advertising. Advertising and selling companies must inform potential customers about the production locations, wages, supply chains, mode of action, history, invention and development. If there is even the slightest indication of risks, potential customers must be informed of these risks. This is to reduce unequal information about a product between producers, traders and customers.

12.6 Global education

In the Knowledge Directory, there is a media library where foreigners can first learn the national language and then take all domestic educational qualifications virtually, no matter where in the world. For this purpose, all necessary content is transferred from the Knowledge Directory to the Internet. Foreigners can order the internet-enabled products of the People's Innovation Company Intranet[164] directly from the media library. These qualifications are only recognised if a real final examination has been passed at a domestic educational institution.

12.7 Knowledge Directory[165]

Each educational content is given a profile on which it can be taught in different forms of presentation. Each subject area, educational qualification or research community is grouped together. All the knowledge that is taught in state educational institutions, provided by the ministries or shared by voluntary users is filed in this directory.

The Knowledge Directory is structured similarly to wikipedia[166]. However, the articles are state-approved. Teachers, auditors from the Company Auditing Agency or other qualified specialists proofread the articles or write them themselves. Each verified article is given a seal at the top of the homepage, indicating which person and organisation verified it and when. This service primarily serves the domestic people, because all knowledge can be accessed via the intranet. Distance learning or further education in detention are thus enormously facilitated. For all of humanity, this means the preservation of global knowledge in a new form that is presumably more accessible to humans than just reading written texts. Free computer programs and construction plans for models from 3D printers are also stored in the Knowledge Directory and can be integrated into production processes via the Labour Directory.

In the Knowledge Directory, a lot of emphasis is placed on working with sources as precisely as possible. In some cases, several footnotes can be included in a sentence, or sources can be indicated by link or ISBN number. Other sources must be

164 Ministry of Digital Affairs - 13 People's Innovation Company Intranet
165 §182.2 Further education: BV Art. 64a
166 https://www.wikipedia.de/

listed under "other".

12.7.1 Profiles

The Knowledge Directory consists of profiles in which the same educational content can be learned in different ways. The content consists of texts, sound recordings, videos, images and Virtual Reality programmes.[167] All content is keyworded so that age groups, necessary vocabulary and learning types can be listed. The assessment of whether Knowledge Directory content is suitable for auditory, visual or haptic learning types is examined by learners and teachers in the educational institutions on the basis of lesson content, examinations, examination performance and survey questionnaires.

The Knowledge Directory can be categorised into different areas. This allows the user to adjust the view of the entire body of knowledge. For this purpose, there are sortings according to scientific specialist department, economic sector, (high) school educational qualification and age.

Those who want to graduate can view the curriculum and all the necessary educational content, study, take digital exams and register directly for the final exam. To do so, examinees simply go to the nearest educational institution offering the degree, present their identity card, prove that they have a digital exam grade point average below 2.0 and take the regular exams there.

Those who want to optimise their company select their economic sector and get helpful knowledge displayed specifically for their company if they allow the algorithm to access the data of the profile in the Labour Directory from the company. This data matching is free of charge for all domestic companies. The intranet is not available to foreigner companies. However, admission via the Internet is possible for foreigners because there is an Internet version of the Knowledge Directory.

167https://www.viscopic.com/ https://www.craftguide.online/

12.7.2 Control and correction

The contents of the Knowledge Directory are controlled for correctness at state educational institutions. At all state educational institutions, it is permitted to submit final examinations as explanatory videos or programmed learning games. This creates a media library of knowledge. This knowledge has been checked for accuracy by teachers, rated and translated from written form into multimedia form by persons in training.

The Ministry of Education gets film crews from the Ministry of Media Affairs[168] to film the entire curriculum taught in all primary, comprehensive and college schools for a year. At the end, every subject is edited together. National language and maths would be the longest films or series because you have them in primary school and you can study both subjects at college.

This programme is being developed jointly by all types of schools, because all contents are to be formulated in a way that is already understandable for primary school pupils. This fact is tested on fourth graders in state primary schools. The learners are only given small sections at a time, which they have to explain in their own words. For this purpose, each fourth grader is given half a year to carry out the training lessons with the help of the People's Computer, Virtual Reality glasses and sensor clothing.

All users who find faults can correct them and the correction is checked by at least 3 teachers before it is published. Teachers receive automatic prompts for this on their People's Computer during their duty period. As soon as 3 teachers agree to the correction, it will be implemented.

12.7.3 Administration

The Knowledge Directory is administered by users and teachers. Users can rate the contributions. Through versioning, one can see the history of changes, what was changed by whom, when and how. If you don't like something, you can change it. Each

---

168 Ministry of Media Affairs - 13.2.2.1 Learning content for degrees

profile has a noticeboard where discussions can be held and questions and answers can be created. There you can indicate what you did not understand or what was helpful.

12.7.4 Assessment test

An assessment test can be used to digitally determine which qualifications one already possesses and which teaching units are still missing in order to achieve a desired qualification or to be able to understand the answer to a self-posed question. The necessary data is retrieved from the user's profile in the Education Directory. For example, fluent and comprehensible reading and writing is a qualification that is achieved with the completion of primary school. If too many faults are detected here in a test consisting of tasks from real written exams, it is recommended to repeat the third and fourth grade in the subject national language digitally via the Knowledge Directory. As soon as all exercises and examinations have been passed with a grade point average of less than 2.0, one can register for the corresponding central performance record at a primary school of one's election.

13 Switching to the new system

13.1 Centralise education system

The regions are no longer responsible for education and are dissolved. All state educational institutions are administered centrally by the Ministry of Education. The institutions are managed directly democratically and the management is elected directly by the members of the affected educational institution.

13.2 Centralise curriculum

The curricula are revised and drafted according to the new curriculum development procedure. Until the procedure is completed for the first time, the current curricula of Bavaria are used. There, the qualifications of students are the best and unemployment is the lowest.

13.3 Changes to the school system

In the first step, schools switch from classes to courses so that learners can choose their teachers by creating their own timetable. In the second step, teachers have to adapt their teaching to the three different teaching methods and determine how to teach a course in voting with the learners. In the third and final step, the new curriculum is imported and the schools between primary school and college are merged into the comprehensive school. All school buildings will be checked to see which courses and certificates can be offered there. In the medium term, some school buildings will be closed and others will be increased so that learners will have to commute less often. Teachers draw up a profile of all the subjects, courses and teaching methods they can offer and report this to the Education Authority.

13.4 Changes in the vocational schools

The vocational schools are continued as vocational training colleges and educational programmes that lead to the same appeal are combined. For example, the educator from the vocational training college and the study of social work at the technical college can work in nursery schools. What is needed here is to abolish the educational programme that specialises less in one profession and more in several professions. In this case, the social work degree programme would take over the contents of the educator degree programme and spin off all areas of care for the elderly or adult education into another degree programme. The new degree programme is called educator.

13.5 Integrating adult education centres into the education system

Adult Education Centres (AEC) will be merged with Education Submissions and administered by the Education Authority. Own premises of the AEC are dissolved as long as all surrounding educational institutions offer sufficient space to hold all events. The AECs are run by voluntary citizens as teachers and they determine the range of courses and thus the curriculum.

13.6 Conversion of the old ministries

For the conversion of the old ministries, all departments and units of the old ministries that are changing to this ministry are identified. The organigrams are used to determine whether an entire department and all its units are changing or only individual units. All unsuitable departments and units are dropped. The existing staff adapts its tasks to the new requirements.

Contact form

Dear reader
If you would like to make what you have read come true, in whole or in part, together with other like-minded people, I offer you several possibilities with this contact form. Fill it out, tear out the page and send it by post to:
Andreas Seidl, P.O. Box 1206, 63488 Seligenstadt / Germany

Or send the details to:
Phone: 0049 1522 818 2243 (whatsapp, telegram, signal)
Email: andreas.seidl2022@web.de

Please mark with a cross:
O   I want to found a dynamic People's Party.
O   I want to donate money for implementation.
O   I want contacts with like-minded people in my area.

Forename: _____

Surname: _____

Please fill in only the contact option through which a reply should be made.

Street, house no.:   _____

Postcode, city, country: _____

Phone: _____

Email address: _____